The Busy Mom's Book of
Preschool
Activities

The Busy Mom's Book of
Preschool
Activities

Jamie Kyle McGillian

Illustrated by Tracey Wood

STERLING PUBLISHING CO., INC.
NEW YORK

Edited by Hazel Chan
Design by Carol Thompson

Library of Congress Cataloging-in-Publication Data

McGillian, Jamie Kyle.
  The busy mom's book of preschool activities / Jamie Kyle McGillian.
  p. cm.
  Includes index.
  ISBN 1-4027-1245-6
  1. Creative activities and seat work. 2. Mother and child. 3. Education,
Preschool–Activity programs. I. Title.
LB1140.35.C74M3 2005
372.13–dc22
     2004005257

10 9 8 7 6 5 4 3 2 1

Published by Sterling Publishing Co., Inc.
387 Park Avenue South, New York, NY 10016
© 2004 by Jamie Kyle McGillian
Distributed in Canada by Sterling Publishing
c/o Canadian Manda Group, 165 Dufferin Street
Toronto, Ontario, Canada M6K 3H6
Distributed in Great Britain and Europe by Chris Lloyd at Orca Book
Services, Stanley House, Fleets Lane, Poole BH15 3AJ, England
Distributed in Australia by Capricorn Link (Australia) Pty. Ltd.
P.O. Box 704, Windsor, NSW 2756, Australia

Manufactured in the United States of America
All rights reserved

Sterling ISBN 1-4027-1245-6 Hardcover
              1-4027-1951-5 Paperback

To my daughters, Bailey and Devan, two little girls who keep me busy and are always game for adventure. Stanley Krolick, my busy dad, who made me want to write books and sing show tunes. And Lisa Tager, my big sister, who always showed me the way.

CONTENTS

Foreword

*Y*ou are your child's first teacher. You are the first to introduce her to words, sounds, and letters. It's your hugs, your gentle voice, your sometimes-silly, sometimes-serious ways and ideas that will teach your child a multitude of skills. With your cues and encouragement, your young child may learn to bounce a ball, hop on one foot, dance the hokey pokey, or sing a silly song. But how can you maximize the fun, the discovery, and the learning while still managing to get the dishes done or finish a report for work?

With an abundance of lively games at your fingertips that teach, entertain, and prepare your little one for the world. You do not need to spend hours hunting for games that will appeal to your preschooler. The activities in this small book will provide you and your little one with endless enjoyment. Each chapter addresses a certain scenario or occasion, so you can turn to that chapter and find immediate ideas. Included are also *Tips for Busy Moms*. You'll also find ways to help prepare your child for school and beyond. As you play, know that you are helping to develop your child's thinking, creative, social, and reading-readiness skills. Isn't that just what every busy mom wants?

First Things First

Whether you're a first-time mom, or an old hand at mother-hood, yours is a busy life. No matter what your age, how many children you have, whether you are a stay-at-home mom, a back-to-work mom, or a back-to-school mom, your days are filled with countless tasks to insure a young child's well-being. And if you have a preschooler (or two or three or four), you are faced with the exciting and sometimes overwhelming challenge of priming your little one(s) for the world. How will you find the time to run errands, make dinner, read aloud, teach the basics, and still breathe? It is very easy to become inundated by the many responsibilities that face you each day. Before beginning with the different activities you can do with your child, here are some *Busy Mom's Daily Survival Strategies* to keep in mind that may help you through your hectic day.

Busy Mom's Daily Survival Strategies

PLAN FOR EVERY OCCASION, EVEN THE UNEXPECTED. Did you ever notice how some moms have it all together? They are ready for any curve ball, mishap, or adventure. They can propose a fun game, whip up a nutritious snack, and turn a pout into a smile at the drop of a teddy bear. These moms take a little time beforehand to plan for every adventure. They are organized. They pack their bag the night before. They make lists. They consult a network of sources and other moms for valuable information.

Planning takes time. So take a little—while you're in the shower, brushing your teeth, or beating your eggs—to think about the details. Ask yourself, "What do I need to pull this off?" Check the weather. Take along a map. Pack a few snacks and drinks. And don't forget to take along this book for instant games and activities.

BE REAL. DON'T BITE OFF MORE THAN YOU CAN CHEW. Which is the smarter plan for a busy mom? (a) Start out at the park with your three-year-old. Then have lunch in an outdoor café, take three pony rides, dash off to a face-painting session, visit the petting zoo, enjoy a super-duper ice cream cone, help your child put on her water wings, jump in the pool, then greet the stretcher that's going to carry you out. (b) Take your three-year-old to the park, grab some lunch, then head home for quiet play and a nap.

You may think the first choice makes for the better mom, but choose the second choice if you want to live. Keep it short and simple. If you take on too much in one day, you may risk tantrums, bad moods, bellyaches, sunburns, and other nasty stuff—not to mention what your child may experience. Plus, how could you possibly top such a day? Less is often more where preschoolers are concerned.

LAUGH AND YOUR PRESCHOOLER LAUGHS WITH YOU. A sense of humor is vital. Finding the silliness in a tense or even impossible situation teaches your young child how to accept, appreciate, and even handle the good, the bad, and, of course, the ugly times.

CALL UPON YOUR SUPER POWERS. You are a mom. You can do virtually anything. If something goes wrong, such as you drive two hours to the butterfly exhibit only to discover that it's open only to butterflies, just trust your mommy powers. Remember, you're a mommy and at least one person in the world thinks you are invincible. Find a local park, bookstore, or pet store and let the good times roll.

REMEMBER YOU? Remember the old days, the B.C. (before child) times when you had the where-with-all to get to the gym on a regular basis, enjoy a manicure, or, heaven forbid, sip a glass of wine or drink a cup of coffee? For those times when you will be exhausted and delirious from being slightly cooped up with your wonderful child whom you love so dearly, stop and remember yourself. If you can't arrange an hour or two for yourself, try the following ideas and activities that will keep your child happy while you do a little something for yourself.

Ten Ways to Take Care of You

1 Put your child in a stroller and get out. Take a brisk walk. Remember people? And how about the smells, the sounds, and the sights? Share your thoughts with your child. Just keep talking and walking. That's instant therapy.

2 If you have a child who is at least two and a half years old, you can do manicures and pedicures. A boy's nails can be trimmed and filed. A girl's nails can also be polished. Be sure to use non-toxic polish. While nails are being filed or drying, count fingers and toes, sing silly songs, and make up your own version of *This Little Piggy*.

3 While playing with your child in a kiddie pool, rub your feet against the cement at the bottom of the pool. It'll work like a pumice stone. Happy exfoliating!

4 Haven't had time for an eyebrow tweezing? Let your child be your helper. He can hold your hand mirror while you tweeze. Turn it into a game of keeping the mirror still. See how long he can keep it still. Praise his concentration skills. Admire your shapely brows.

5 You and your preschooler can give each other hand and back massages with fruit-scented creams. Turn it into a game. You can "write" a letter or shape on a child's back and he can guess the letter or shape. Your child can "draw" pictures on your back. Ahh, your skin is moisturized and you've had a massage from your favorite little person.

6 Play your music. If you're like most moms of young children, you're already exposing your child to the wonders of music, but chances are it's mostly kids' music. Share your favorite tunes and as you enjoy your music, invite your child into your arms. Dance around and be yourself. Now you have the music that's always meant so much to you and your little treasure. Life is good.

7 Multitasking again? This time, while you make dinner and sing nursery rhymes with your little

one, mix a little olive oil with a dab of perfume into your hair for an instant conditioner. Rinse it off in your evening shower. (Evening showers may not be something you can count on, but when you have olive oil in your hair, you'll have an evening shower!)

8 While you gently push your child on the swing, do Kegels, the exercise that helps reduce leaking urine before and after childbirth. Squeeze your pelvic-floor muscles tightly. Hold for ten seconds. Then release and repeat at least ten times at a stretch. Smile.

9 Go to a kid's movie. While your child is entertained, you can meditate, make a wish list, or take a nap.

10 Enjoy the company of other moms who can related to your daily challenges. Organize a mom's club and have a monthly night out. Share child-rearing strategies, swap time-saving recipes, have a book chat, or tell jokes. Invite the moms you meet at the playground, in play groups, or even at the pediatrician's waiting room.

CHAPTER 1

Getting a Head Start for School

NURSERY RHYMES

Young children and their caregivers have shared and enjoyed traditional nursery rhymes for hundreds of years. They are wonderful words and melodies to recite while swinging on a swing, walking through the woods, or even going through the drive-thru. Learn five of them and sing them to your child at different points of the day. In just a short time, your child will learn the words and will be able to sing them with you. Consider "Hickory Dickory Dock," "Little Jack Horner," "Baa! Baa! Black Sheep," "Jack and Jill," and "Lavender's Blue."

SILLY SONGS

After teaching your child basic nursery rhymes, enhance the fun and learning with your own rhyme songs. Pick a tune and write some silly words. Encourage your child to help you rhyme. Here's a song about the moon that you can sing at the park or in the car. It will put everybody in a good mood almost instantly.

Silly Moon Song

Let's have a party,
Let's invite the moon.
Let's do it in April, May, or June.
You bring the punch and I will bring the lunch.
Let's have a party and celebrate the moon.
Sing, dance, and play and act just like a loon.

* * * * * * * *

RHYME GAME

Say a word and then ask your child to come up with a word that rhymes with that word. If your child needs your help, give three or four possible choices and let the child choose the rhyming word.

RHYME TIME

When you read rhyming books, try letting your child complete the rhyme by pausing a moment before reading the rhyme. Can he guess the rhyming word?

RHYMING FUN

Make up silly nursery rhymes with your child. Try this one out:

I am a nutty Mama
I like to have my fun
I like to skip and jump
And then I like to run.

Now repeat the verse, but let your child fill in the third line with two new verbs. Be as silly or as serious as you want. Keep the first, second, and fourth line the same and you'll still have the fun of a rhyme.

LETTER SOUNDS

Spend time saying the letters and making the sounds of each letter of the alphabet. While you're strolling through town, or playing in the sandbox, ask your child to repeat the sound.

LETTER PLAY

- Shoe box
- 1 cup of sand or salt
- Straws

Give your child a shoe box and fill it with sand or salt. Guide a child's index finger, or give your child a straw and gently guide her hand, to create each letter of the alphabet. Ask your child to identify each letter. Then have her write the letters by herself.

LETTER GAME

Recite the alphabet. For each letter, challenge your child and yourself to come up with a word that begins with that letter.

LETTER OF THE DAY

You and your preschooler can celebrate a letter of the day. Write the letter with a crayon, a stick in the sandbox, or chalk on the sidewalk. Talk about the letter's sound and tell what words begin with that letter. Point out the letter during the day whenever you see it on signs, books, and grocery products. At the end of the day, have your child talk about the letter. When this game becomes familiar, you and your child can play Number of the Day.

GIVE A CHEER

Pretend you're a cheerleader and spell out words from traffic signs. Shout, "Give me an S, give me a T, give me an O, give me a P. Now what do you got? STOP." Move your arms and legs to add to the fun. Then give your child a chance to cheer and spell.

GOING ON A PICNIC

Play variations on the game, "I'm going on a picnic and I'm going to bring—." Introduce your child to the sounds of the alphabet. If you say, "Apple," ask her to think of another word that begins with the same sound. If this is too challenging, turn it into a memory game, where each player must repeat everything from the beginning to the end.

NUMBER COUNTS

After you teach your child to count from 1 to 10, show her the numbers and as you count, point to each one.

NUMBER TALK

Spend some time during the day thinking about numbers. Look at page numbers. Look at the numbers on a phone and on a clock face. Say the numbers that belong to your home phone or the numbers of your child's birthday.

FIST OF PENNIES

Give your child a fist of pennies to count. Make up word problems, such as "If I give you two more pennies, and you give me back three, how many do you have?"

CLIP-ART FUN

Make several copies of simple clip art from computer programs or black-line coloring books. Cut out the pictures into small squares. Use the squares to give your child practice saying the word for each picture. Show him assorted squares and have him identify the pictures. For each right answer, award him with a sticker. Or, cut out two of each picture, line the squares up in a game-board style and turn it into a memory game. Can your child find the matching pairs?

SIZE ORDER

Give your child three different-sized objects, such as a paper clip, a rock, and a hat. Have him put the objects in size order. Ask which is the smallest item? Which is the largest?

THE RIGHT LID

Save plastic lids and containers of all shapes and sizes. Remove the lids from the containers and have your child put the correct lid on each container.

MATCH IT

Gather some ordinary objects, such as a fork, a key, a nail clipper, and a wristwatch. Then trace each object. Have your child match the real object to the outlined item.

SORT

Give your child a chance to sort small objects by giving her several empty wipe containers and have her separate the items. She can sort a pile of toy cars, pennies, marbles, and blocks. This activity may also encourage a child to clean up.

COLOR PLAY

Name a color and have your child point to something in the room that is that color. Cut magazine pictures out and ask your child to find certain colors.

SHIP SHAPE

Call out shapes to your child and identify them wherever you are. Then point to the shape and ask your child to identify it.

SORT IT

Cut up magazines and catalogs. Help your child sort the pictures into categories such as food, cars, people, flowers, or clothing.

POINT TO IT

As you read to your child, point to the words as you pronounce them.

KNOCK-KNOCK

Be a star in your child's book. Make up knock-knock jokes with her.

OUT AND ABOUT

Point out printed words in and out of the house. Talk about signs, logos, and menus.

ME BOOKS

- Paper
- Crayons and markers
- Photos
- Old magazines
- Paste
- Scissors
- Staple

Your child can create a book about himself. Create the pages with all the things that make your child special: family portraits,

* * * * * * * *

photos, and drawings of favorite things. You can add key words to each page. When the book is complete, staple the pages along the left edge. Have your child share his book with family and friends. Talk about each page and read the key words.

BAG OF WORDS

Use a brown bag from the grocery store and fill it with index cards that have words written on them. Group the words so that they all have to do with one theme: going to the beach, going to school, staying safe, or taking a trip to the doctor's office. Let your child pick out one word at a time. Read each word to your child. Let him identify the letters. Then talk about the words and what they have to do with one another.

SCRIBBLE BOOK

Give your child small pads or writing paper. Encourage her to draw or scribble on them. Then have her tell you what she has written.

ABC BOOK

After sharing some alphabet books with your child, create your own. Use a colorful binder. For each page, write the letter and a word that begins with that letter. Ask your child to think of a word that begins with that sound. Then the two of you can draw the pictures together. As your child develops her skills, she can update and add on to her ABC book.

FIRST WORDS

Make a scrapbook of first words. Your child can draw the picture of each word and you can write the word.

BOOK OF MOODS

As your child learns about emotions, take the time to make a book about being happy, sad, mad, scared, silly, shy, and frustrated. When he is happy, have him draw a picture of that happy feeling and you can write a corresponding story. When he is sad, have him draw that feeling and you can help get the words on paper. Try to use the book as a way to talk about feelings.

* * * * * * * *

WHAT'S MISSING?

Draw simple pictures with something missing: a house with no windows, a cat without a tail, a face with only one eye. Ask your child to tell you what's missing and then have her finish the picture.

ABOUT THE BOOK

Share the name of the author and illustrator with your child when reading a book. Let him gain a sense of the artist's or author's style by spending a few minutes talking about the pictures and the words. Ask your child to describe the pictures and the words.

BOOK CHAT

How can you make the books in your child's library fly off the shelves and into your child's mind? By talking about elements from the stories when you're not reading them. Repeat a popular phrase from a story. For example, when trying a new food, ask your child if she will eat it in a house, eat it with a mouse, and so forth (Dr. Seuss' *Green Eggs and Ham*). Or, talk about a situation from a book. For example, ask your child what he would do if he were a bird and he hatched while you were away from the nest? How would he find his mom? What would he do? (P.D. Eastman's *Are You My Mother?*)

Or, "walk through" the pages of a favorite story, put yourselves in the adventure, and try to create your own outcome.

* * * * * * * * *

FAMILY NEWS

Write a family newsletter with your child. Send it out to the relatives at holiday time. Share big events. Is there a new baby to celebrate?

SCHOOL HOUSE

Play school. Give your young child a preview of school concepts, such as working together, listening, and getting a feel for what may be expected of her. Take turns with your child being the teacher and student.

PRESCHOOLER'S PLANNER

Make and keep play dates, keep track of appointments, and count the days until the next holiday or party with a colorful cork board in your child's room. Include a section for a weekly or monthly calendar. Let your child decorate it with stickers. Also, hang photos and your child's artwork.

COLOR DAY

Learn the colors of the rainbow and have fun declaring color days. For example, on Green Day, wear green clothing, eat green foods (like green grapes, celery slices, and broccoli soup), and make sure to draw pictures of green things.

CONCRETE POEMS

Write concrete poems with your child. To create one, arrange

* * * * * * * *

the words in a way so that a picture forms. For instance, a poem about a star might be written in the shape of a star. Hang the concrete poems in your child's room or on your refrigerator.

IN SHAPE

Draw a bunch of different shapes. Point to each one and have your child name the shape. She can also trace each shape.

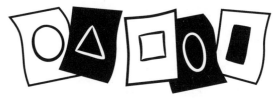

ALPHABET MAGNETS

- Colored markers
- Plain white mailing labels
- Old magnetic business cards

Turn old magnetic business cards into alphabet magnets. Cover each magnet with a mailing label. Write one letter on each magnetic tile. Keep the alphabet magnets low on your refrigerator so that your child can play with them anytime.

ART OF TALKING

Make talking fun by using play phones and having silly conversations with your child. Identify yourself as the Tickle Monster or the Belly Kisser, then give your child a chance to do the same. If you don't have play phones handy, use your child's foot.

While speaking on one foot, you could say, "Hold on, I have another call," and then switch to the other foot phone.

THIS LITTLE PIGGY

After you do this one by the book, do it again, but make up your own nonsense stories. Put your child's name in place of piggy. Of course, end it the same way—with a tickle.

SIGN IT

Check out books on sign language and teach it to your self and your child. It's a great skill to have under your belt, and your child will love communicating with you in this special way.

NOISE DETECTIVE

Listen to the sounds of cars, trucks, birds, dogs, children, and lawn mowers. Ask your child to describe each noise. Ask him to tell you which noises he likes and which ones he doesn't.

HAPPY, HAPPY

Make a happy box for your child. Fill it with stickers, rubber stamps, photos, markers, and other small items. Take a visit to the happy box whenever your child needs a lift.

CAN I QUOTE YOU?

Keep a small notebook of the clever things your child says. When something you hear that makes you smile, laugh, or cry, the both of you can quickly jot it down. Your child, as he develops further, will get a kick out of it—and so will you.

WHISPER IT

Sometimes, just for fun, talk to your child in a whisper. Pretend a baby is sleeping close by. Can you and your child understand each other's whispers?

READING SPACE

Design a cozy reading spot with your child. Maybe the space is the corner of your den, or simply a comfortable chair by the front door. The idea of the space is to create a reading-friendly atmosphere with plenty of light, enough room for two, and accessible reading material. That may mean a basket of board books and magazines, a soft blanket, and pillows.

GO OUTSIDE

Now that you have your indoor reading spot, can you and your child design a cool outdoor reading space? Even if you can't really do it, talk about it or have your child draw it.

BIG EARS

Help your child become a good listener. Ask him to close his eyes and listen carefully. Tell him a story using a quiet voice. Use rich descriptive words in your story, such as "The big fat hen wore a red silk bonnet and sat on a tiny wooden bench,

waiting for her friend, the purple spider." Then ask your child
questions relating to the story: What color was the bonnet?
What was the hen sitting on? What color was the spider?

LIBRARY TRIP

When you go to the library, look for books that tap your child's
interest. Also, share books that relate to things that are happening in your child's life, such as preparing for a new sibling,
facing a fear, learning more about favorite types of animals.

HAPPY HALF

Celebrate a child's half-birthday with a half a cake, half of a
happy birthday song, and half the amount of candles. Use the
event as a way to introduce the calendar. Review the names of
the months of the year. Have your child count the months.
Happy half.

BLOCK COMMANDS

Challenge your child with two or three different-colored blocks.
For example, ask her to put the red block on top of the blue one
or place the yellow one under the green one. Use words like
"above," "in back of," and "next to" to teach her the placement
of things.

*   *   *   *   *   *   *   *

the both of you can quickly jot it down. Your child, as he develops further, will get a kick out of it—and so will you.

WHISPER IT

Sometimes, just for fun, talk to your child in a whisper. Pretend a baby is sleeping close by. Can you and your child understand each other's whispers?

READING SPACE

Design a cozy reading spot with your child. Maybe the space is the corner of your den, or simply a comfortable chair by the front door. The idea of the space is to create a reading-friendly atmosphere with plenty of light, enough room for two, and accessible reading material. That may mean a basket of board books and magazines, a soft blanket, and pillows.

GO OUTSIDE

Now that you have your indoor reading spot, can you and your child design a cool outdoor reading space? Even if you can't really do it, talk about it or have your child draw it.

BIG EARS

Help your child become a good listener. Ask him to close his eyes and listen carefully. Tell him a story using a quiet voice. Use rich descriptive words in your story, such as "The big fat hen wore a red silk bonnet and sat on a tiny wooden bench,

* * * * * * * *

waiting for her friend, the purple spider." Then ask your child questions relating to the story: What color was the bonnet? What was the hen sitting on? What color was the spider?

LIBRARY TRIP

When you go to the library, look for books that tap your child's interest. Also, share books that relate to things that are happening in your child's life, such as preparing for a new sibling, facing a fear, learning more about favorite types of animals.

HAPPY HALF

Celebrate a child's half-birthday with a half a cake, half of a happy birthday song, and half the amount of candles. Use the event as a way to introduce the calendar. Review the names of the months of the year. Have your child count the months. Happy half.

BLOCK COMMANDS

Challenge your child with two or three different-colored blocks. For example, ask her to put the red block on top of the blue one or place the yellow one under the green one. Use words like "above," "in back of," and "next to" to teach her the placement of things.

GROWING UP

- Poster board or piece of wood
- Markers
- Glue
- Fabric

Make a growth board with your child. Use poster board or a wood board that's five-feet tall. Decorate it with markers or cover it with fabric. Attach a measuring stick or draw one onto the board with markers. Measure your child every few weeks. Then let him measure his feet, his hands, and his waist.

COLLECTIBLES

Encourage your child to take up a collection. Choose from collectible toys, seashells, action figures, buttons, postcards, or key

chains. Decide where to display the collection and how to store it. What can your child learn about her collection?

CREATIVE THINKING

Help your child become a creative thinker by asking "what if" questions. *What if the sky fell? What if the moon could talk? What if it rained candy?* Write a story with your child using his responses.

BOOK TALK

Ask your child to read you a favorite story. Let him describe the pictures. Ask him what each character is doing.

OFF THE PAGE

Let your child retell a favorite story using words or by drawing a picture.

MAKING PATTERNS

Make patterns with different everyday objects. Use various lids from food jars. Gather other objects, such as buttons, colored paper clips, stickers, and coins to create simple patterns. Ask your child to talk about the pattern, then continue it.

PATTERN PATROL

Point out other patterns on clothes, home furnishings, and gardens. Let your child point out the patterns he sees.

✳   ✳   ✳   ✳   ✳   ✳   ✳   ✳

BOOKS THAT HEAL

Keep a small collection of about three or four favorite books that soothe your child. Keep them in a handy basket and use them whenever your child needs a little lift. Get your child into the habit of reaching for a book to feel better.

WRITING TOOLS

Keep a writing box on a low shelf in your child's playroom or play area. Fill the box with paper, pencils, erasers, washable crayons and markers, and stickers.

NAME GAME

Get to know names with your child. Start the game by giving your child a choice of three names. He has to decide which name he would choose as his own. Then he can give you three names to choose from. Use this as an opportunity to say the names of all the children that your child comes into contact with.

PEOPLE IN THE NEIGHBORHOOD

Talk about the people who work in your neighborhood: the store cashier, the gas station attendant, the police officer, the lifeguard, the firefighter, and the pizza delivery person. Talk with your child about the responsibilities of each job.

STORY WRITER

It's not too early for your child to write a story, play, or poem

✳   ✳   ✳   ✳   ✳   ✳   ✳   ✳

with your help. You can start by updating a fairy tale or pretend to be a dynamic character, such as Curious George, and get in all kinds of trouble. Ask your child, "What might happen if you were George and you tried to make a surprise dinner for the man with the yellow hat?"

NOVEL IDEA

Glue an envelope into your child's favorite books. Store useful ideas, anecdotes, and activities that relate to the book in the envelope. Those ideas will come in handy later, especially if another sibling comes along.

COIN GUESS

Hide a coin under one of three small cups. Move the cups swiftly, changing the whereabouts of the coin frequently. Ask your child to guess which cup has the coin under it.

COUNTING ON TV

Watch your child's favorite television show with her and make it a counting occasion. How many animals are featured? How many characters are there? How many different pairs of shoes do you see?

SKILL BUILDER

Boost your child's literacy skills by showing him that you are a reader. Let him see you reading the newspaper, magazines, books, and catalogs. Show him the print on each.

BOOK ON TAPE

You and your child can record yourselves reading a favorite book. (Your child can make the sound effects.) You can play the tape before bed and let your child follow along with the book in hand. Also, use the tape when you have a baby-sitter and are unable to put your child to sleep yourself.

POST-IT MEMORY

Make a memory game by using Post-it Notes and a pencil. Scribble shapes, numbers, or letters on the sheets. Draw two of each. Lay the Post-its facedown. As each player uncovers a

matching pair, she collects the post-its. The player with the most matching pairs wins.

POSTCARDS FROM HOME

Use your own personal postcard collection to stir your child's imagination. Talk about exotic and faraway places. Show your child where each place is located on a map or a globe. Try to write an adventure to go with the postcards.

CLAP IT OUT

Get your child aware of the syllables in each word by clapping each sound. How many syllables does the word "mommy" have in it? Clap once for "mom" and once more for "my." That makes two syllables.

✳ ✳ ✳ ✳ ✳ ✳ ✳ ✳

TIPS for BusY MomS

◎ Make time to enjoy your little one as well as yourself. Get in touch with the little kid you were. (It wasn't that long ago, you know.) The laundry can wait. Now is the time to get on all fours, act like a lion, and roar. Your child will love you for it.

◎ Do things with a young child that you don't otherwise take the time to do. Bake cookies from scratch. Let your tot crack the eggs, even though you know you'll have to spend a few minutes picking out the shells.

◎ Always be prepared. Young kids always leave their battery-operated toys on and drain the batteries. Keep a stash of batteries on hand.

◎ Buy scented bags for dirty diapers. They will prevent stinky smells from getting the best of you.

◎ Make coupons for really good behavior: healthy snacks, a walk with Mommy or Daddy, a back rub, a book read, or time on your lap. Use the coupons anywhere and anyhow.

◎ Don't ever feel guilty. You might feel you gave your first child more "mommy time" than you gave your second or third child. Or you might feel badly because you took a weekend away with your girlfriends and your child came down with a fever. It's never going to go exactly as you planned, but don't waste precious time feeling guilty. Instead, relish the moments and remember how lucky you are.

CHAPTER 2
The Daily Grind

GOOD MORNING

Say good morning to your young child in a special way. Make your voice deep, high, or spooky. Say good morning in several languages. Say it without words. Just make it joyful.

GREET THE DAY

Start each day off right with a song or nursery rhyme that the two of you can sing together.

GREET THE TOYS

Let your child say good morning to her favorite toys. Bring on the gift of gab by encouraging her to ask them how they slept and how they are feeling.

GREAT EXPECTATIONS

What's on for the day? Give your child a rundown so he'll have some idea of what to expect. Let him know if he'll be seeing a playmate, going to the park, or shopping for some gardening tools at the local nursery.

WEATHER CHECK

Get your child thinking about the weather. Look out the window together. Listen to the weather report on the radio. Is the sun shining? How warm or cold is it? Pretend you are your child's very own weather reporter and talk about what kind of clothes she'll need to wear. Then give your child a chance to be your weather reporter and let her help you figure out what to wear.

DAYS OF WEEK

Have your child learn the days of the week by setting aside some time each day to name the day. Write it down on a small chalkboard or a piece of paper. As your child becomes fluent with the days of the week, have him tell you what day it is.

BREAKFAST COUNTS

Teach your child that breakfast is an important meal by making time for it every day. Sometimes, when you're not pressed for time, you can make it special by being a funny waitress or cook. On special days, treat your child like a queen or a king by serving up breakfast on a silver platter.

MORNING MEETING

Have breakfast chats and talk with your child about positive behavior. Praise the good stuff. This is an ideal time for siblings to talk about issues.

MEALTIME COMPANY

A reluctant eater may surprise you if she can sit next to her favorite stuffed animal at the table.

PHOTO TIME

Show your child photos of family and friends. This is a great wind-down activity, and it will help your child learn names and places.

TV TIME

Make morning TV time an occasion to get up and sing, dance, clap, and talk with your child about what's happening on the show.

TALKING

Talk to your child about what makes him feel better when he's sad. Is there a special toy or song that can comfort him? Tell him what helps you feel better. Try out a hug or a picture book.

SAD FEELINGS

Let a child know that we can't always feel happy twenty-four hours a day. Tell her that it's all right to feel sad, to cry, and to talk about those sad feelings. Let a sad child be for a few minutes. Then, remind him to get happy with a happy song, a tickle, or a stretch.

NEED A LAUGH

Help a child in need of humor with a laugh book. Fill it with favorite jokes, riddles, cartoons, and silly family stories.

GET UP

Is your child having a tough time waking up? Sing, "Head, shoulders, knees, and toes" to the tune of "London Bridge." Use your hands to point out the body parts. Don't forget to include eyes, ears, mouth, and nose. Sing the song slow or fast.

TIME FOR SHARING

We all know how difficult sharing can be. Every time your child shares a prized possession with a sibling or friend, acknowledge it by recording it in an *I Shared Today* book. Write down the details and then reread it to your child.

HAVE A JUMP

Let your child have a few jumps on the bed before breakfast. It will wake her and delight her. Make it a rule that you have to be in the room for the jumping.

ABC FUN

When you're child has her alphabet down, make it extra fun by having her recite it while standing on one foot or jumping rope.

TIME FOR A TICKLE

Make time for a tickle break. Work out a routine. Tell your child that Ticky the Tickle Queen is in town and she will be making a stop at your house. Let your child enjoy the anticipation of Ticky's arrival. Then unveil Ticky (your hand) and give him a little tickle. Give your child a chance to pretend he's Ticky. Let yourself be tickled by your child.

HEAD GAMES

Prepare for a child's first trip to the hairdresser by playing barbershop with your child. Explain that you are the hairdresser. Let your child wear a smock and sit in a chair. You can spritz her hair with a water spray bottle, or just brush it. This fun experience may just alleviate all haircutting related fears.

DRESS UP

As you and your child get dressed for the day, name your child's clothes items: shirt, socks, pants and so on. Also name your child's body parts. Encourage her to repeat the words. Soon she'll be a pro at these words.

FASHION SHOW FLAIR

Have a fashion show with the new clothes you and your child have for the coming season. Let her practice buttoning, zipping, and snapping on her clothes. Make a space for the runway. Roll out a red towel. As the fashion model flaunts her stuff, the rest of the family can admire her clothes and pretend to snap photos.

BUTTON SENSE

Teach your child to button his shirt from the bottom up. That will make it easier to match the buttons with the buttonholes.

LACING UP

Help your child learn to tie shoelaces by giving him a shoe to practice on. It may be easier for him to practice lacing up a shoe that isn't on his foot.

TIPS for BusY MomS

◎ If it breaks your heart when your little one outgrows a special shirt or hat, don't give it away yet. Let a cherished stuffed toy wear it for a while.

◎ Use a hanging canvas shoe bag on the back of a closet door to store your child's specialty items, such as hair clips, swim goggles, hats, and mittens.

TALK TO ME

Help your child talk about what he did during a play date or at play group by asking specific questions such as, "What did you have for snack? What toys did you play with?"

MICROPHONE DELIGHT

Give a young performer a microphone and let her sing and dance about the highlights of her day.

HELLO, GOOD-BYE

Make your good-byes and hellos really special with a fun ritual. Try a cool handshake. Use your right hands and touch pinkies, then rub thumbs together and spin around.

HAPPY CHAIR

In your child's playroom or bedroom, make a happy chair: a comfy seat that's got pillows, ribbons, bows, and streamers attached to it. Make this a place to read, nap, or snuggle.

TEN WAYS TO MAKE FOOD SHOPPING FUN

1 Before writing a shopping list, have your child help you determine what you need to buy by checking the cupboards, refrigerator, and freezer. Ask questions like, "Do we have any butter? Do we need more milk?"

2 As you write the list, say each item out loud and then point to the word so you're your child can see it in print. Whenever possible, write the word and draw a picture of the food item.

3 When you arrive at the market, let your child hold your shopping list and a crayon. Have him cross off each item on your list as you put it in the cart. Your child can also be your coupon holder.

4 Have your child help you find an item. Pretend it's some

kind of treasure hunt. Praise him each time he recognizes letters, shapes, and colors.

5 Identify all the fresh fruits and vegetables in the produce section. Let your child touch and smell the cucumbers, onions, melons, oranges, and the other items that you purchase.

6 Let your child help you weigh your produce items with the small produce scale at the market. Ask which weighs more, a tomato or a melon?

7 As you walk the aisles, explain which items of food are from which food groups. Explain that cereal belongs in the

breads and grains group, yogurt belongs in the dairy group, etc. As your child becomes familiar with the food groups, challenge him to match the food to its food group.

8 Every once in a while, let your child choose the flavor of the yogurt or the type of cheese to buy. Later, when you eat it, compliment him on his selection.

9 At the deli counter, let your child hold the ticket. When the deli person calls your number, have your child answer.

10 Talk about all the goings-on in the market. What's happening outside the store? Are big trucks delivering any items? Are there other children in the store? Is the store crowded? Is there a worker at the counter whom you've met before? Turn the weekly shopping into a fun social experience.

TIPS for BusY MomS

◎ Make a weekly meal plan on Sundays. It will save you time in the long run.

CANDY JAR COUNTDOWN

How many days to a birthday, a family party, or a big event? Help your child get a grasp on the time frame by filling a jar with the same number of candies as there are days remaining to the event. Each day have a countdown treat.

✳   ✳   ✳   ✳   ✳   ✳   ✳   ✳

FIRST-TIME BOOK

Commemorate big first-time events, such as using the potty, reading books, brushing teeth, and riding a two-wheeler. Take a picture, or have your child draw a picture, and write some of the details about the big accomplishment. Keep it in a binder and add it to a bigger memory book of notable events for your child.

PHOTO DESIGNER

Keep a photo board going in your child's bedroom, her play-room, or the kitchen. Every few weeks, update the board together. Let your child help you choose the best photos and think of captions to go with the photos.

POTTY POWER

Potty training is a major accomplishment. Celebrate it with your child with a "Bye-Bye Diaper" party. Cheer the end of poopie diapers. Let your child take a bow.

UNIQUE THANK YOUS

After your child's birthday party, make thank-you notes to her friends. Let your child put her finger- or her handprint on a solid note card with a bright color paint. Then attach a photo of your child opening the gift, enjoying her birthday cake, or blowing out her candles.

RELAX

Help your child unwind. Have him get comfortable on the floor. Have him close his eyes and say to him, "Think about your feet. Squeeze your toes together. Hold the squeeze. Hold, hold, and hold. Now let the toes go." Continue doing this for his legs, fingers, neck, and mouth.

PEANUT BUTTER STRETCH

Take a stretching break with your child. Put on slow music. Then tell your child to curl up with you in the shape of a peanut. Slowly begin to stretch out as if the peanut butter is spreading out onto the bread. Extend the arms, legs, and torso until both of you are all stretched out. Then assume the peanut position again.

TRANSITION TIMES

Just finished a lively game of catch or tag? Help your child switch gears with a quiet activity: read a book, fold laundry, or open the mail.

FREE TIME

Give your child a few minutes of downtime. Let her choose her own activity. If she needs prompting, suggest putting her doll down for a nap, dusting a plush toy, or looking at pictures.

FOUR WAYS TO TEACH TABLE MANNERS

1 Throw a tea party with your child's toys. Demonstrate the best table manners. Praise your child every time she displays good manners.

2 Create a story about a stuffed toy that has terrible manners, then have your child teach him everything he knows.

3 Make a book about good table manners with your child. She can draw the pictures and you can write the words. You can share the book with relatives.

4 Write out the rules to good table manners and post them in a playroom. When your child has a playmate over, you can review the rules for good manners.

GOOD BEHAVIOR GAME

Help your child understand good and bad behavior by turning it into a game. Talk about the difference between the two behaviors. Then use the day's events to identify what good behavior is and what it is not.

SIX WAYS TO TEACH SPECIFIC GOOD MANNERS

1 Teach your child that name-calling is never acceptable by creating a scenario in which the two of you are children. Pretend that one of you is a name caller. Practice telling the name caller that put-downs are not acceptable. The name caller can apologize and try to make the other person feel better. You can also create other scenarios in which you or your child knock something over, spill something, or run into someone and say, "Excuse me," "It was an accident," or "I'm sorry."

2 Teach your child to say "please" and "thank you" by turning them into magic words. During snack time, if he wants a cookie, he has to say, "please" in order to get one and "thank you" once he gets it.

3 Play being sick and have your child mimic you coughing and sneezing into a tissue. Explain to her that people do this because they don't want other people to catch their icky germs. When she does have a cold, she will know to cover her mouth.

4 Have a "Cleaner Hands" competition with your child after he uses the bathroom and before eating. Use kid-friendly liquid soaps to make it more fun.

5 Make a Soft Voice/Big Voice game. The rules are you will only respond to your child indoors if she talks softly. Once you two are outdoors, you can talk in a big voice.

6 Role-play the possibilities of when it is alright to interrupt an adult. Pretend you are the child and your child is the adult. Have him pretend that he is having a grown-up talk with someone. Wait for a pause in the conversation to say, "Excuse me," in a nice voice. Explain the reason for your interruption. Follow up with a smile.

BEHAVIOR MANAGEMENT

Create a secret signal or phrase to let your child know that you are not happy with his behavior in public. Try "chicken fric-a-zee" or snap your fingers twice. Explain in advance that that is a warning to stop whining, crying, or acting unreasonably.

ROLE PLAY

Ask your child what she would do in the following situations. Use each as a springboard to talk about appropriate behavior.

1 You drink a cup of juice and burp out loud. What should you do?

2 You spill paint on Daddy's T-shirt. What do you do?

3 You accidentally step on a friend's foot in the park. What should you do?

4 You want a drink, but Mom and Dad are talking. What should you do?

PRAISE GOOD MANNERS

Make rewards to give to your child when she shows good manners. You can give your child a certificate for her good manners.

SIX WAYS TO CULTIVATE FRIENDSHIP

1 Sit with your child and compile a list of rules for making friends. Include what you should do: be nice, act friendly, share; and what you shouldn't do: hit, be bossy, and bite.

2 Use puppets or other toys to model how good friends talk to each other, how they listen, and how they share with one another.

3 Play songs about friendship.

4 Read books about friendships.

5 Talk about the good friends that you have. Explain how important a good friend is.

6 You and your child can interview good friends and ask them questions about what makes their friendship special.

INTO THE BATH

Reluctant bathers will be more willing to soak it up if they have a special water toy, a squishy bath book, or company in the tub.

You and your child can make up your own bathtub adventures about magic soap bubbles and soft rubber duckies.

COMPANY IN THE BATH

Let your child select one or two bath toys from the bath-toy bin each time she takes a bath.

TOY BRUSHING

Brush a doll's or a toy's mouth before bedtime to stress the importance of brushing your teeth and taking care of them.

THE DOCTOR/DENTIST IS IN

Play doctor and dentist with your child to ease his fears. This will also give him practice in talking about where it hurts and when it hurts.

MOON BEAM

Make moon watching a nightly activity. Observe the moon's shape and ask your child to describe it. Finish it off with a book about the moon, or tell your own lunar story. Before bed, imagine with your child what it feels like to walk on the moon, then take a "moon walk" to bed.

WISH UPON A STAR

On a clear night, wish upon a star with your child. Share your wishes out loud. Talk about the many kinds of wishes people have.

FLASHLIGHT FRIEND

Before going to sleep, let your child shine a flashlight in all the corners of his room to make sure he is safe, to say goodnight to his stuffed toys, and to play shadow games right before bed.

SILLY MAGIC

Pretend to take something magical or silly out from your child's pajama pocket or sleeve before she goes to bed. What's in there?

Coupons for happy dreams? Pancakes for breakfast tomorrow? Wet kisses for under her neck?

STORY CHOOSER

Can't decide which story to read before bed? Fill an empty plastic jar with small strips of paper that have your book titles written on them. Let your child shake the jar, then choose a story by picking a title from the jar. Turn this into a nightly ritual.

NIGHT, NIGHT

Before saying good night to your child, say a prayer, sing a lullaby, or simply say, "I love you." Whatever it is, make sure it's simple, comforting, and fun enough to do every night. Let your child know he's safe and he's loved.

TIPS for BusY MomS

◎ If you promise your child a trip to the library or the park, know that she is going to hold you to it. Don't promise what you can't deliver.

CHAPTER
3

Kitchen
Encounters of
the Fun Kind

WASH HANDS

Before working in the kitchen with food, wash your hands with your child. Let your child stand on a stool by the kitchen sink and wash your hands together with soap and warm water. Say the ABC's while you wash.

QUICK APRON

Make an apron with your child for him to wear. Use a dishtowel or a clean burp cloth. Attach a string or a shoelace to both sides of the cloth and tie it around his waist.

WHISK IT

When you're making scrambled eggs, let your child beat the eggs with a small wire whisk.

MIX IT

Let your child mix the cookie batter when you're baking or stir the homemade chocolate pudding in the pot.

PANCAKE PARTY

Make pancakes with your child. She can help mix the batter, fold in the chocolate chips, and pour syrup on a cooked pancake.

SMASH IT

Let your child crush boiled potatoes to make mashed potatoes. She can also add the butter and the milk and mix it all together.

☆ *Kitchen Encounters of the Fun Kind* ☆

STIR IT

Hold your child's hand while carefully stirring a pot of gravy, sauce, or soup. Reward him with a taste.

TONG TIME

Let your child experience the joy of kitchen tongs. Have her use them to transfer small items from one bowl to another.

TOSS IT

Let your child help you toss a fancy salad when company's coming. You can chop all the salad pieces and she can arrange them in the big salad bowl and help you mix in the dressing.

☆ *Kitchen Encounters of the Fun Kind* ☆

MEASURE FOR MEASURE

Show your child a large measuring cup. Let him help you fill it to measure a cup of milk, a half of a cup of flour, or a third of a cup of oil.

KITCHEN FUN BOX

Store a shoe box filled with neat stuff for a young chef to discover. Keep the box in a low drawer or cupboard that your child can easily reach. Fill the kitchen fun box with wooden spoons, plastic dishes, an apron, sheets of tin foil, plastic play food, dishtowels, plastic containers, and measuring spoons. Try to change

the contents of the box every week so that it remains fresh and exciting to your child.

☆ *Kitchen Encounters of the Fun Kind* ☆

☆ ☆ ☆ ☆ ☆ ☆ ☆ ☆

FRUIT SAMPLER

Have your child identify the different fruits. Ask her their name and color. You can also ask her to describe the texture of the fruit. Is it mushy, crunchy, or wet?

WASHING FRUIT

Let your child help you wash pieces of fruit. Dry them with a paper towel and then place them in a large bowl.

FRUIT SALAD FUN

Let your child help you make a fruit salad. After you have cut a few different fruits, let him try to match the cut pieces with the whole fruit.

FRUIT ARRANGING

Have your child arrange the fruit slices onto a colorful platter. Ask her to count the pieces.

FRUIT PATTERN

Have your child make a pattern using the different pieces of fruit, such as green grape, pineapple chunk, apple slice, watermelon, and green grape again.

FRUIT FACES

Make fruit faces with your child. Use a sliced strawberry for the mouth, grape halves for the eyes, and orange pieces for the nose.

☆ *Kitchen Encounters of the Fun Kind* ☆

FRUIT ON A STICK

Make fruit kabobs with fresh or canned fruit: strawberries, banana chunks, grapes, and melons. Snap off the sharp skewer points.

GUESS MY FRUIT

Pretend you're a fruit and give your child enough clues until she guesses what you are. Say, "I'm thinking of a fruit. I am yellow and long and eaten by monkeys." Then show her the banana and give her a taste.

SNACK SHAPES

Prepare and enjoy a shapely snack. Cut cheese into triangles. Munch on square-shaped crackers. Cut melon into small circles. What fun!

VEGETABLE FACES

Make vegetable faces with sweet red pepper slices for the mouth, a zucchini triangle for the nose, peas for the eyes, and broccoli or grated carrots for the hair.

CARROT

Let your child peel a carrot with you, then eat it like a bunny.

☆   ☆   ☆   ☆   ☆   ☆   ☆   ☆

CELERY TREAT

Have your child stuff a celery stick with peanut butter or cream cheese. Then top it with raisins or sunflower seeds.

GELATIN JIGGLERS

- Non-stick cooking spray
- 2 large boxes of gelatin
- 2 1/2 cups of boiling water
- ABC cookie cutters

Make alphabet gelatin pieces to teach your child his ABCs. Stir the boiling water into the gelatin. Pour the mixture into a 13 x 9 inch (33 x 23 cm) pan coated with non-sticking spray. Chill for at least 3 hours. To cut the jigglers, dip the bottom of the pan into warm water for 20 seconds to loosen the gelatin. Have your child help you make each letter by pressing the cookie cutters all the way through. Lift with a metal spatula. Makes at least two dozen jigglers. Before your child eats the letter, have him call it out.

BE WAITED ON

Let your child wait on you. Give her a supply of plastic plates and plastic foods. Use the experience to model good manners. Next time, you can wait on her.

CANDY MATH

You can do simple math problems with your child with raisins, nuts, or goldfish crackers. Let your child count and do simple additions and subtractions.

MATH MUNCHING

Make mealtime a math activity. Have your child count the number of bites it takes to eat a slice of pizza. Ask, "How many seeds are in a slice of watermelon?" or "How many sips of milk do you have left in your cup?"

CUT IT

Allow your child to slice a banana with a plastic knife. Count the number of slices. How many will your child eat? How many will you eat? Turn it into a number game.

PIZZA PARTY

Have a pizza party and teach your child basic fractions. Show your child what half a pizza looks like and what a quarter looks like.

SPONGE HELP

Give your child a clean, damp sponge to wipe the dusty plastic containers in your cupboard.

SORT CANS

Let your child help you rearrange your food cabinets. Let her help you sort the items. Ask her to put the boxes together or line up all the cans.

WASH, WASH

Let your child wash some plastic cups and dishes with a sponge, soap, and water.

TASTE TESTING

Gather some of your child's favorite foods. Blindfold her and have her identify each food. Have her describe the different tastes and textures. Then ask her to group these foods categories: sweet, salty, bitter, sour, spicy, or tangy.

CHEERIOS TOWER

Stand a single strand of uncooked spaghetti in a small lump of clay. Have your child thread Cheerios, one by one, without breaking the spaghetti strand. Turn it into a competition. Who has the longest Cheerios tower?

LEMONADE, ANYONE?

- 8 cups of water
- 12 tablespoons of lemon juice
- 1 1/2 cups of sugar
- Ice cubes

On a hot, summer day make a pitcher of lemonade with your child. Mix the water, lemon juice, and sugar together in a large pitcher. Chill and taste. Add more sugar or lemon, if needed. Then enjoy a nice glass while the both of you sit outside.

MAKE TEA

- Four or five herbal tea bags
- Large jar
- Water
- Ice cubes
- Lemon slices

Make citrus-flavored herbal tea with your child. Place the tea bags in a large jar and fill it with water. Seal the jar and leave it outside on a sunny afternoon for a few hours. Add ice and lemon slices, then enjoy.

ICE POPS

- Craft sticks
- Fruit juice
- Small paper cups

Fill each cup three-fourths full with juice. Put them in the freezer. After about 45 minutes, take out the cups and have your child place a stick in each. Freeze again for about 3 hours. When the pops are frozen, just peel off the paper cups and enjoy!

☆ *Kitchen Encounters of the Fun Kind* ☆

CRACKERWICHES

Set out crackers with various toppings—cheese, turkey pieces, and peanut butter—and have a make-your-own-snack day.

PEANUT BUTTER BUSINESS

- Peanuts in the shell
- Food processor
- Small jars

Make peanut-butter presents with your child. Shell the peanuts with him. Place the nuts into your food processor and grind until smooth while he watches. Put the peanut butter in small jars. Attach stickers, ribbons, or homemade labels onto the jars. Give them as gifts to people who do not have peanut allergies.

BAKING SEEDS

- Pumpkin seeds
- Salt
- Cookie sheet
- Sealed container

Soak pumpkin seeds in salty water for a few hours. Drain, then spread on a cookie sheet. Have your child sprinkle the seeds with salt. Bake in a preheated oven at 350° for about 20 minutes. Store the seeds in a sealed container.

TIPS for BusY MomS

◎ While you're in the kitchen, take time to talk to your child about the kinds of special dishes your mom made you when you were young. Share with him stories about holidays and festive occasions that you celebrated.

◎ During holiday time, take the time to include your child in the food preparation. Create your own food traditions with her input.

☆ *Kitchen Encounters of the Fun Kind* ☆

CHAPTER 4
Help Around the House

*   *   *   *   *   *   *   *

TOYS AWAY

Sing a song or play music when playtime is over and clean-up time is to begin. Help your child pick up and put away toys. To make it fun, have your child pick up all the blue things first, then the red things, the round things, and so on. Store the toys in bins, crates, and easy-to-reach shelves.

BEAT THE CLOCK

Using a kitchen timer, create a race to see if your child can beat the clock in picking up his toys.

HAMPER TIME

Have your child throw the dirty clothes in the hamper and help you carry it to the washing machine.

SOCK SORTER

Let your child sort and match socks.

SHOE STACKER

Keep a shoe rack by your front door. Let your child help you organize the shoes on the rack each day.

NAME TIME

Teach your child to write his name. Then he can write it on the labels that you secure in his clothing.

FINE FOLDER

Teach your child how to fold towels, dish rags, and clothes. Each time you fold, count. Then give him a chance to show you what he's learned. Let him count the number of folds for each item. Praise his folding and counting skills.

DUSTER

Have your child use a feather duster or damp cloth to dust the furniture. Keep breakables from her reach.

SWIPER

Let a child wipe a counter space with a damp sponge.

WINDOW WASHER

Give your child a spray can of water and some paper towels. Let her help you wash the windows.

CAR WASHER

Your child can help you wash the car. Get a bucket of soapy water and some rags, and let the fun begin.

WEEDER

Invest in a small pair of gardening gloves for your child. Have her help you pull weeds. Explain the difference between plants and weeds.

WATERING

Let your child water the plants inside and the garden outside. This is a grown-up task that children will love to do.

FLOWER ARRANGER

When you have fresh flowers, let your child help you make beautiful arrangements. Talk about the types of flowers, the various colors, and smells.

BATTERY ASSISTANT

Let your child help you replace batteries in a toy. Pretend that you are Doctor Battery. Let him test out the toy to see if the batteries are working.

PHONE BOOK

Let your child create a phone book of special friends and family. Paste a photo of each person in the book and write his or her telephone number next to it. Whenever your child wants to chat to one of her phone book friends, you can look up the number together and then dial it together.

MAIL SORTER

Have your child help you sort the mail, especially during holiday season when mailboxes are often overstuffed. Show your child how to read the mailing label and help him distribute the letter or package to the right people at home.

BED MAKER

Give your child a chance to make the beds with you every morning. Let her help you smooth out the covers and prop the pillows.

PILLOW FLUFFER

Your child can help you freshen the pillows in your living room and bedrooms.

RECYCLER

Make your child be your official recycling assistant. She can help gather the newspapers from the rooms of the house, pile the aluminum cans in a recycling bag, and tear pieces of paper and cardboard.

DINNER BELL RINGER

When it's time for dinner, let your child ring a bell and call everyone to the table.

DINNER HELP

After dinner, let your little one carry a dish from the table and load it in the dishwasher.

CHORE CHART

Post a chore chart on a wall. When your child finishes his chores, he can check it off, or put a sticker on the board. A chart with a lot of check marks could warrant a small reward.

TIPS for BusY MomS

◎ Don't worry if you don't get all the housework done. Nobody ever went to their grave thinking, "I should have spent more time cleaning."

FIVE WAYS TO TEACH A CHILD RESPONSIBILITY

1 If your child is not allergic to animals, get a pet and show her how to take care of it. Have her accompany you as you walk it, feed it, and take it to the vet. Help her see what taking care of an animal really entails so that by the time she's a teen, she'll be up for the job.

2 Give your child a daily task—setting the table, checking the answering machine for messages, sponging the table—and let him do it everyday. Try to get him to do the task without your prompting. Give him pointers where there's room for improvement. Praise him for his good work.

3 Let your child in on the daily responsibilities of parenthood by reversing roles. Challenge your child to be the adult and name the many jobs a mom or dad has.

4 On the next "Take Your Child to Work" day, have your little one accompany you to the office so that she can see what mommy does.

5 Let your child choose a hobby, such as gymnastics, dance, or swimming, and work on every aspect of it with him. Give him support if he becomes frustrated. Praise him when he sticks to it.

CHAPTER
5

Outside Explorers

EXPLORERS

Explore the outdoors with your child. Observe colors, textures, smells, and sounds. Look for living and non-living things and help your child differentiate between the two.

SUNSET

Watch a sunset with your child. Afterwards, ask her to put it into words or try to draw it in a picture.

BAG IT

Let your child collect branches, acorns, leaves, shells, and rocks into a brown bag. When you return home, have her spread out her collection and examine each object. Ask her to describe each item in her collection.

BIRD WATCH

If you've got a young dinosaur lover, tell her that some scientists believe that birds are modern dinosaurs. Ask your child how are birds and dinosaurs are alike. Bring binoculars so that she can check out the different eyes, wings, and claws.

FOR THE BIRDS

- Toilet paper cardboard roll
- Crisco shortening
- Craft stick
- Bird seeds
- Some yarn

Have your child help you make a bird feeder. Using a craft stick, coat the cardboard roll from a toilet paper with Crisco shortening. Roll it in a mixture of birdseeds. Attach a piece of yarn on opposite ends. Hang it in a tree and watch the birds come for snacks.

SMELLY TREES

Let your child find a leaf from a tree. Crush it in your hands. Now smell your hands. Explain to your child that some leaves smell musty; others smell like pine, fresh or sharp. Go on a smelling spree.

LEAP OF LEAVES

Leap with your child into a pile of freshly raked leaves. Crunch!

BE GRASSY

Find a slight and grassy hill where both of you can roll down.

SUNNY PRINTS

Place items like pencils, erasers, coins, or rocks on a black piece of construction paper. Place it in direct sunlight. At the end of the day, remove the items and observe the sun prints. Turn it into artwork.

COLOR FUN

Draw a rainbow on the sidewalk with colored chalk. Then ask your child to hop on yellow, jump on blue, and sit on green. Turn it into a "Simon Says" game.

TRACE YOURSELF

How big are you compared to outside creatures? You and your child can trace each other on the sidewalk with colored chalk.

How much bigger are you than a frog? How much bigger is your child than a bird?

SQUIRT FUN

Fill a few small squirt bottles with water. Let your child use it to water indoor and outdoor plants, spray the sidewalk, or, on hot days, have a squirting match with you. The winner is the one who is the driest.

RAINBOW

Make a rainbow on a sunny day. All you need is lots of sunshine and fine spray from your garden hose. Spray the hose upwards and look for the rainbow.

WATCH BUILDING

The next time you see a construction site, spend a few minutes watching it. Explain to your child what's going on.

CAMP OUT

Build a fort for you and your child by hanging blankets over chairs. Give your child a flashlight and a pile of books and spend the afternoon reading in your fort.

CLEAN THE POOL

In warm weather, fill a wading pool with all kinds of things: leaves, rocks, twigs, folded paper. Then give your child a net and let her clean the pool.

ROCK DANCE

Let your child jump, dance, and run on a bed of rocks. Make sure she's wearing sneakers and guide her along the rocks so that she is safe.

SEEDS FOR THOUGHT

Show your child a selection of seeds: in a tomato, an apple, an orange, a watermelon. Explain that each seed can grow to a thousand times its size.

DANDELION WISH

Find a dandelion. Let your child make a wish and blow it into the breeze. Tell him not to tell you what he wished for.

TURNING SOIL

If you're planting a garden, switch off letting your child turning the soil.

SUNFLOWERS

Plant beautiful sunflowers. They're easy to grow and young children will enjoy standing next to such tall flowers. She can compare her height to that of the flowers.

✳ ✳ ✳ ✳ ✳ ✳ ✳ ✳

GROWING PHOTOS

Make a photo record of the flowers you and your child planted. Take pictures of them every week or so to follow their growth.

PLANT BULBS

Plant bulbs in the fall. Choose from daffodils, crocus, and tulips. Your child can help by dropping the bulb into the hole.

ANTS AROUND

Learn about ants with your child. Observe an ant hill. Place a small piece of food nearby and watch the ants gather. You can also buy an ant farm and enjoy watching them this way.

WASH UP

After gardening, have a "Cleaner Hands" competition with child. Wash your hands with kid-friendly liquid soap.

BUG TRACKS

Get down on all fours and watch a bug with your child. Examine the insect with a magnifying glass.

BUG DETECTIVE

- Magnifying glass
- Butterfly net
- Jar with small holes
  punched in the lid.

Help your child catch bugs in your garden. Put it in a jar so it can't escape. Ask your child to describe what he sees. Maybe he can draw a quick picture of it. After he has had some time observing it, set it free and find a different bug. Encourage him to tell Daddy about his bug detective skills.

PET SPIDER

Trap a spider in a jelly jar, then transfer it into a large glass container, such as a pickle jar. Place some soil, a few upright twigs, leaves, and a capful of water in the jar with the spider. Punch several small holes in the lid so the spider can breathe. Put the jar in a cool, dry place away from direct heat and light. Observe.

LADYBUG CHEERS

Honor the ladybug. Tell your child that she's an asset to the garden because she eats many garden pests as well as being harmless and friendly. Count the number of spots on each ladybug that you find.

FIREFLIES APPROACH

Attract fireflies at night by keeping a flashlight pointed to the ground so that the light isn't too bright. Turn the flashlight on and off with the same rhythm of the firefly: 1 second on, 2 seconds off.

LETTERS IN SNOW

Make pictures in the snow. Or you can call out the letters of your child's name and see if she can stomp out each letter.

TEN THINGS TO DO AT THE BEACH

There's so much to do with a young child when you're at the beach. Remember these ideas next time you're by the shore. Unfortunately, rest isn't on the list.

1 Fly a kite.
2 Look for living creatures and observe them.
3 Collect rocks and shells.
4 Build a sand castle.
5 Get wet.
6 Pour a bucket of ocean water over your favorite little person.
7 Walk, skip, or jog along the shoreline.
8 Pretend that you are cave people.
9 Enjoy a picnic.
10 Let yourself be buried in the sand. (Hey, it gives you a few minutes on your back!)

CHAPTER
6

On the Road

RULES OF THE RIDE

Before embarking on your road trip, write down a set of rules. Share the rules with your child.

RED LIGHT, GREEN LIGHT

Have your child call out the color of the traffic lights. Whenever he sees a red light, have him call out, "Red light." When the light turns green, have him call out, "Green light." Ask him to keep count of the number of red and green lights he sees.

CHALK IT UP

Keep a small chalkboard in the car. As you drive to your destination, your child can practice making shapes, letters, and numbers. For a handy eraser, use an unwanted shoulder pad.

BRIDE'S GAME

Each person takes a turn to call out either something old, something new, or something blue. Another adult in the car can keep score by giving a point to each person who finds something from one of the categories. If a person finds something from two of the categories, such as a new blue car, that person gets two points. When a person gets ten points, she yells out, "Bride's Game," and the game starts again.

STEERING WHEEL

Give your child a small wheel or Frisbee and let her steer the car from her seat.

YUM, YUM

Make cereal necklaces and bracelets with colored yarn and ring-shaped cereal. On long car rides, your child can snack on her cereal jewels.

DRIVING TOOLS

Involve your child in the trip by providing a map, pencils, a compass, and a note pad so that he can follow the journey.

ZOO BOOKS

Make a trip to the zoo extra special by taking a photo of each animal you see. Create an A-to-Z zoo book. Help your child put the pages in alphabetical order.

LISTEN WELL

Play books on tape in the car. Then have family discussions about the stories you've heard.

QUICK PRIZE

Packstickers, small toys, and games in a sealed plastic bag. Use the items as prizes or quick pick-me-ups on long car rides.

HELP IN AN INSTANT

Give your two to four year old your keys, a drinking straw, an empty water bottle, a compact mirror, or a baby wipe. He will usually be actively engaged with it.

LICENSE PLATE ACTION

Read license plates. Identify colors. Compare pictures. Point out numbers and letters.

TIPS for BusY MomS

◎ Take a trip to the dollar store to buy a bag of small toys. Next time you're traveling, instead of spending a small fortune in souvenir shops, let your child have a pick in your special toy bag.

BINGO

Make bingo cards by writing simple letters, numbers, and shapes on index cards. Give each passenger (except for the driver) a card and a crayon. As you call out the numbers, shapes, and letters, each player circles what you said on his or her card. When a player has circled out an entire line—either up, down, right, left, or diagonally—he calls out Bingo.

MAZES YOU MAKE

Make a booklet of simple mazes for your child to do while you're driving. Each maze can be drawn with a thin black marker and can have a theme, such as the castle of happiness or the candy palace.

CIRCLE TIME

Draw a page of overlapping circles. Give it to your child. As you drive, ask him to count out the number of circles, trace them, and then draw something using the circles in his picture.

TRUCK FIND

Look for trucks on the road. Every time you find one, ask your child what she thinks is inside the truck. Count the number of wheels. Find out where is the truck is from by looking at its license plate.

* * * * * * * * *

A FEW OF MY FAVORITE THINGS

You and your child can take turns calling out your favorite
things. Pick a category such as food, fun places, or fun things to
do. Here are a couple of example of favorites:

Food

You: Hot cinnamon buns.
Your child: Pizza with sausage.
You: Coconut ice cream.
Your child: Peanut butter.

Fun Places

You: Swimming pool.
Your child: The beach.
You: The movies.
Your child: The garden.

AFTER THE TRIP

Let your child use the vacation map as the background for a colorful collage, highlighting the places you went and the things
you did on your trip. Attach souvenirs, photos, and other
objects, such as postcards, receipts, and ticket stubs. Mount it on
a colorful poster board and hang it in your child's room.

* * * * * * * *

SEVEN WAYS TO EAT OUT WITH YOUR CHILD

Dining out with young children is not always an easy task. Sometimes, it can bring on heartburn even before your meal is served. But with a little planning, you may actually find it a pleasurable experience.

1 Help your child prepare for the event by telling her that you are going to a restaurant and that she needs to be on good behavior. Go over the rules with your child. Let her know that there is only talking in soft voices, no getting up from the table, no crying, no pointing or staring at other people, and absolutely no whining. You may want to mention that this is also a table manners test and offer to give her a best-behavior prize sticker, a back-scratching, or a special dessert if she shows proper table manners.

2 Talk about favorite foods. Ask your child what her favorite dish is and ask your child how she would prepare it from start to finish.

3 Use the menu as an opportunity to let your child show you what she knows. Have her identify letters, words, shapes, and colors.

4 Carry crayons and paper or a small coloring book in your bag. If you have a few kids at the table, have an art contest. Ask the children to create the ultimate game room or pictures of things that make them happy.

5 Bring along a family of quirky characters you created by draw different faces on craft sticks. Let your child walk

*   *   *   *   *   *   *   *

them on the table and have them pretend to be playing in the playground or skating on a pond.

6 Carry small books, toys, and crafts. Use pipe cleaners to keep your child busy and happy with endless craft possibilities. A small doll, plush toy, or a sticker book also make great options.

7 If you don't have anything else to entertain your child, let her play with a clean napkin. She can fold it into different shapes. She can scrunch it up and pretend that it is something magical. Ask your child to imagine the napkin coming to life. What life form would it be?

CHAPTER 7

Nurture the Budding Artist

BOOK IT

- Scissors
- Hole punch
- Fabric squares
- Yarn

Have your child make her own tactile book. Use a variety of fabrics: silk, satin, faux fur, corduroy, burlap. Cut the fabrics in small but even squares. Punch three holes down the left side of each fabric square and tie a piece of yarn through each. Let your child flip through the pages of the book and describe the texture of each page.

SILLY STRAWS

Cut heart shapes or animal shapes from colored construction paper. Cut two slits in the middle of each shape, about 1 inch (2¹/2 cm) apart, and slide the straws through the slits.

* Nurture the Budding Artist *

FAMILY OF PUPPETS

Make color or black-and-white photocopies of family headshots. Cut out the faces from each photo and paste each onto a craft stick. Decorate each character with scraps of fabric.

CORKY CHARACTERS

- Wine corks
- Pipe cleaners
- Cotton balls
- Markers

Make a family of corky characters with your child using the above materials.

PLAYING IN THE SNOW

It's snowing and your child isn't feeling well enough to go outside and play. Do the next best thing. Take a cookie sheet, throw on a mound of snow, and let your child play.

SMALL RUBBINGS

Tape the four corners of a piece of paper to a work surface. Slide a small object, such as a coin, key, or charm, under the paper. Lightly rub over the area with a pencil or crayon to see its print.

* * * * * * * *

A NEW SCENT

Fill an empty baby food jar with a few flower petals, water, and a few drops of rosewater to make homemade perfume. Decorate the jar with stickers.

PUZZLING

Back your child's masterpiece with cardboard. Cut the picture into six large pieces to make an instant puzzle. Store it in a sandwich-sized plastic bag.

PHOTO OPPORTUNITY

Weeks before the holidays, take photos of your child so that you can use the pictures to make cards.

STEPPING STONES

Gather a variety of large rocks. You and your child can spray paint them and then use them as stepping stones in your garden. Let your child plan where the rocks should be.

ROCK WITH A FACE

Who said rocks don't make good pets? Let your child find a good, solid rock. Have her draw a face on the rock. Name the rock and give it a nice home, like a place on your child's bookshelf.

*   *   *   *   *   *   *   *

ROCK PAPERWEIGHT

Let your child decorate a rock with markers, paints, glitter, stickers, and use them as paperweights or doorstoppers.

FLANNEL BOARD FUN

Don't throw away your child's worn-out flannel blanket. Recycle it into a colorful flannel board. Staple the blanket onto a large cardboard surface. Cut out characters and shapes from other pieces of colorful flannel and make up stories or tell nursery rhymes using appropriate shapes and characters.

UNDERSTANDING COLORS

Make a rainbow and ask your child how each color makes him feel. What color is happy for him? What color is sad?

PAPER CHAINS

Make paper chains from loops of colored paper.

PIPE CLEANERS

A few packages of different-colored pipe cleaners can provide hours of fun. Make silly 3-D characters. Or glue the pipe cleaners to construction paper in the shape of a house, tree, or bird.

COLLAGE

Make paper collages. Use black paper for the background. Paste scraps of colored tissue paper, colored construction paper, newspaper, and tin foil to the black paper. Let your child put the glue on each piece of paper with a craft stick.

PAPER CUTOUTS

Make paper cutouts of balloons and attach yarn for the balloon string.

IN BLACK AND WHITE

Make beautiful art by pasting white cutouts onto black construction paper. Draw the outlines of trees, flowers, buildings, or clouds.

PUNCH IT

Using a hole punch, let your child make holes in scraps of paper. Let him use the punched-out holes as colored confetti.

TOY SCARVES

Help your child prepare her dolls and stuffed toys for a cold winter by making scarves for her tiny friends. You can use fabric scraps or your child's old clothes.

*   *   *   *   *   *   *   *

BE SHARP

Let your child sharpen a pile of pencils using a manual pencil sharpener. It may not seem like a big deal, but to a young child, it will be a fun accomplishment.

SOAPY BUDDY

- Soap bar
- Washcloth
- Thread
- Sewing needle
- Scissors
- Piece of felt

Make bath time a blast by making a silly, soapy character to help a child lather up. Wrap a washcloth around a bar of soap and sew all four ends together. Cut out facial features from a piece of felt and sew them onto the washcloth. Let your child help you make these soapy buddies for siblings and friends.

PAPER CLIP NECKLACE

Give your child a pile of different-colored paper clips and help her create a colorful necklace by linking the clips together.

SCRAPBOOK FUN

When making a child's scrapbook, cut up some of the cards that your child receives. The words and pictures will enhance the pages.

COOKIE JARS

- Empty coffee can
- Magazines and papers
- Glue
- Shellac

Make a cookie jar with your child using a clean, empty coffee can. Simply cover it with pretty scraps of paper or magazines. You can shellac it to add a nice sheen.

SAND ART

- Colored sand
- Containers
- Stick

Colored sand is sold at most craft stores. It's inexpensive and nontoxic. Your child can make beautiful sand sculptures in glassware, clear containers, fish tanks, and even empty plastic soda containers. Simply have her pour one layer of colored sand at a time. Use a stick to create a pattern in the sand along the inside walls of the container.

* Nurture the Budding Artist *

*   *   *   *   *   *   *   *

TREASURE

- A small, empty plastic soft drink bottle
- Sand
- Glitter
- Beads
- Marbles

Pour sand, glitter, beads, and marbles into a plastic drink bottle. Lay it sideways. Have your child tell you a story about how she came upon this treasure and what it means.

MUFFIN SUPPLIES

Turn an old muffin pan into your child's supply container. Fill each hole with small items, such as stickers, erasers, beads, paper clips, and more. Label each hole with him.

SPRAY PAINT

- Newspapers
- Food coloring or tempera paint
- Water
- Several old spray bottles
- Large sheets of poster board or butcher paper

Create different-colored mixtures by combining water with food coloring or tempera paint. Fill old spray bottles with the different colors. Cover a large work area with newspapers. Spray

the paint on large sheets of poster board or butcher paper. If you're using colored water, spray the sidewalk or driveway to make a greeting card or "Welcome Home" sign.

SQUIRT PAINTING

- Newspapers
- Tempera paint
- Plastic sandwich bags
- Glitter
- Construction paper or poster board

Cover a large work area with newspapers. Pour a little tempera paint into a sandwich-size plastic bag. Add some glitter. Seal the bag. Snip a teeny hole in the corner of the bag, then paint on a poster board or construction paper.

SALT PAPER

- White paper
- Watercolor
- Salt
- Spray water bottle

Dampen a piece of paper. Let your child paint the paper with one color of watercolor. Then sprinkle salt on the page. Let it dry. See how the salt seems to "eat away" at some of the color? Brush off the extra salt. To flatten the paper, dampen it slightly

*   *   *   *   *   *   *   *

using the spray bottle. Protect it in between two sheets of paper and let it sit under a heavy book for a few hours.

TIME IT

Make a time capsule with your child on his or her next birthday. Fill a shoe box with assorted memorabilia: newspaper clippings, photos, a note you wrote to your child, a small toy, a favorite book, a special baby outfit. Seal everything inside the box. Wrap it in colored paper. Decide when your child should reopen the box—on her tenth, twelfth, or fifteenth birthday. Store it in the attic until then.

CHILD'S MAILBOX

- Empty round oatmeal box with a lid
- Colored paper
- Masking tape
- Markers

Make a child's mailbox by covering the box with colored paper. Secure the seams with masking tape. Have your child write his name on the mailbox in big letters. Then teach him to write "MAIL" on the lid. Tape the lid to the bottom of the box so that the lid can open and close.

* Nurture the Budding Artist *

* * * * * * * *

DRUM

- Empty round oatmeal box
- Gift wrapping paper
- Scissors
- Long piece of ribbon
- Wooden spoons

Make a drum by covering empty round oatmeal box with gift wrapping. Punch two holes near the bottom of the box. Have your child thread the ribbon through. Measure how long the ribbon should be so that your child can comfortably hang the drum around her neck while she is marching. Tie. Let her use wooden spoons for drumsticks.

HARP

- Shoe box lid
- Six different-sized rubber bands
- Crayons and markers

Decorate the inside of the lid with crayons and markers. Then stretch the rubber bands around the edges about 1 inch (2½ cm) apart. Have your child carefully play it. Maybe he can make up a song.

*   *   *   *   *   *   *   *

MUSICAL SHAKERS

- Empty film canisters or small yogurt containers
- Beans, rice, macaroni, pebbles, or buttons
- Heavy tape
- Paper
- Crayons

Make shakers by filling the empty film canisters or small yogurt containers with beans, rice, macaroni, pebbles, or buttons. Cover with them with paper. Seal it with heavy tape. Decorate them with crayons. Shake away.

SHOE BOX DOLLHOUSE

- Nine shoe boxes
- Paper clips or staples
- Nontoxic paint

Dollhouses are a lot of fun, but they can be very expensive. Before you make that investment, see how your child does with one by making her own from spare shoe boxes. Stack three boxes across and three boxes on top. Attach the boxes to each other with paper clips or staples. You and your child can paint the shoe boxes and decorate them in many ways. Cover empty individual-sized cereal boxes with paper to create beds and furniture. Make a rug from a carpet sample. Use fabric scraps to put some color into the house.

*   *   *   *   *   *   *   *

ME PILLOWS

- Squares of fabric
- Cotton balls, old socks, or cut-up shoulder pads for stuffing
- Glue
- Needle and yarn
- Felt

Have your child design a special pillow for nap time. Make the pillow with two squares of fabric. Sew the edges, all around, leaving a 2-inch (5-cm) space to stuff the pillow with cotton balls, old socks, or shoulder pads. Sew it closed. Cut out your child's initial in felt and glue or sew to the pillow.

TIPS for BusY MomS

◎ Bored of the same child-friendly places in your area? Check the yellow pages for any toy and train museums, comic book museums, and entertainment museums nearby. Planetariums are another great place to go.

CRAFTS FROM AROUND THE WORLD: OJOS DE DIOS

- Two twigs or craft sticks
- Different-colored yarns
- Glue

Meaning "eyes of God," this ornament from Mexico is not only colorful, but it is a good luck piece as well. Help your child make one by making a t-shape with two twigs or craft sticks. Tie them together at where they cross with yarn. Create a diamond pattern by wrapping different-colored yarns around each arm as you work in a circular motion. When you have reached the ends of the sticks, glue the end of the yarn to the end of each stick.

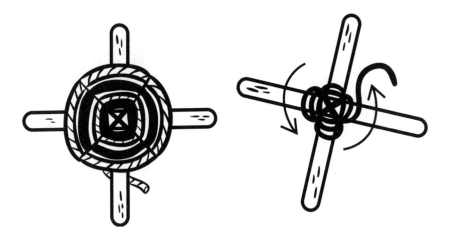

* * * * * * * *

CRAFTS FROM AROUND THE WORLD: KACHINA CRADLE DOLLS

- Assorted cardboard tubes
- Colored paper
- Glue
- Aluminum foil
- Feathers
- Markers
- Pipe cleaners
- Cotton balls
- Fabric scraps

The Hopi and Zuni Indians, who live in the mountains of Arizona, believe that the Kachina dolls, which hang over a baby's bed, bring luck. They can be made from cardboard tubes of various sizes: toilet paper rolls, paper towel rolls, and thin tubes from wire clothes hangers. You and your child can make a family using the different sizes.

Cover each tube with strips of colored paper or color them in with markers. Roll some aluminum foil into a ball to make the doll's head. Glue the head to one end of the cardboard. Draw a face and then decorate the head with feathers, pipe cleaners, cotton balls, and fabric scraps.

* * * * * * * *

ANIMAL MASKS

> • Paper plates
> • Yarn
> • Glue
> • Felt scraps
> • Elastic string

Make simple animal masks with paper plates. Use yarn for the whiskers, scraps of felt for the eyes, ears, nose, tongue, beak, etc. Staple elastic to the sides of the plate.

SLIPPER PUPPETS

Don't throw your child's fuzzy slippers out. Transform them into puppets by dressing them up with fabric scraps.

DOORKNOB DANGLERS

> • Instant photo camera with film
> • Colored poster board
> • Glue
> • Yarn
> • Hole punch

Help your child prepare for a party by making doorknob danglers as cute party favors. Take instant photos of each guest that will be coming. Back each photo to a colorful piece of poster board. Punch a hole at the top of the sheet and tie a piece of colored yarn through the hole. Find a doorknob and let it hang.

ART INTERPRETATION

Take a piece of colored construction paper. Fold the paper in half. Open the paper and, on the fold, pour a small amount of white paint. Fold the paper over the paint. Open it and let it dry. Ask your child what the white paint looks like. Is it a crab, a happy face, or a sea horse?

WRITE ON

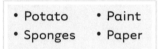

- Potato
- Sponges
- Paint
- Paper

Make sensational stationery with potato or sponge prints. Cut off the end of a potato or cut a sponge into several squares. Have your child dip the potato or sponge into paint and then press it onto a piece of paper. For best results, have him vary the pattern by pressing hard and softly into the paper.

SPONGE ART

Cut some sponges into different shapes: a star, a diamond, or a circle. Show your child how to dip the sponge into a container of nontoxic paint. Dab it on scrap paper and then sponge it on construction paper.

APPLE PRINTS

In the fall, go apple picking. Use spare apple slices to paint with. Dip the apple slices into the paint to make wrapping paper for the holidays.

*   *   *   * *   *   *   *

NATURE ART

- Flowers and leaves
- Clear contact paper
- Scissors

Arrange the flowers and leaves on the sticky side of the contact paper. Cover it with the second sheet, sticky side to sticky side. Trim it with scissors and hang it by window. You can also trim it down to size to make a unique bookmark.

FALLING LEAF

Cut out a large leaf shape. Let your child sponge paint it with yellow, orange, and red paints. Attach a piece of colored yarn to the leaf. Your child can use the leaf to pretend she is a falling leaf. Sing to the tune of London Bridges, "Colored leaves are falling down, falling down, falling down. Colored leaves are falling down...."

TIPS for BusY MomS

◎ Turn your child's artwork into bookmarks, place mats, party invites, or instant wrapping paper.

◎ Make real postcards from a child's artwork. Paste them on to index cards. Make sure to leave a blank space for the recipient's name and address.

CHAPTER 8
Act Up!

* * * * * * * *

BE MY ARMS

Kneel in front of a mirror with your arms behind your back. Have your child stand behind you and stick her arms through to be your arms. Tell a funny story and have her use her arms and hands to tell the story. Add another pair of arms for added fun.

PUPPET POWER

- Old socks
- Markers
- Colored yarn
- Glue

Work out bad feelings with homemade sock puppets. If your child is having difficulties or worries, talking directly to him may not be as effective or easy as working out issues through characters. Explain to your child that Mrs. Easy Sock likes to help and can solve most problems. Encourage him to share his problem. To make the puppet, use a plain sock. Draw a face on it and glue on some yarn for the hair.

*   *   *   *   *   *   *   *

TIGHTROPE WALKER

Have your child walk a pretend tightrope. Have her stretch out her arms and hold her head up high. Applaud as she walks.

BE NATURAL

How would it feel like to be fire? How would water act? And, if you and your child were pretending to be air, what kind of movements would you make? Become each of the elements: earth, wind, fire, and air.

RAIN

Be the rain. The next time it's pouring outside, encourage your child to wiggle her fingers as if they are raindrops. First, be a gentle shower, then pick up speed and become a thundering storm. Incorporate scarves and rainmakers (dried beans in a pie pan). Make up a rain dance to perform for Daddy and the grandparents.

STORMY WEATHER

You be the ship in a storm and let your child be the sailor. Lie down on your belly. Let your child rest over you and hold you at your sides. Shake your body back and forth, up and down. She has to hold on and hang in there. Can she weather the storm, or will she fall into the sea?

IN THE MUD

What would it be like to be stuck in the mud? Imagine you can't move your feet because they're stuck. How will you make your way out of the mud pile? You and your child can pretend to be slogging through a pool of mud. You must cross it and make your way to safety.

BE A STATUE

Show your child statues in your neighborhood, in art books, or on the Internet. Then go to the park and be statues. Find a space, strike a pose, and hold it.

SCARF CREATURES

Fill a bag with colorful scarves. Turn on the music and, one at a time, have each performer grab a scarf from the bag and incorporate it into a dance. Wrap the scarf around your shoulders like

* * * * * * * *

a magical cape. Cover your head with it and turn yourself into a dancing troll. Twist it into a tail and be a bunny. Wiggle it high, wiggle it low. There's no limit to the creative movements you can make.

SITUATION COMEDY

It's time for some improvisation. You can help your child and his friends set the scene by telling them a set of unusual circumstances. Try this: Your child is a librarian and you are a talking dinosaur and you've come to the library to find a book about friendship. The dinosaur has to ask the librarian for help finding the book, but the catch is the dinosaur can't talk. She can only make grunting sounds. Let the group act out the situation.

TALENT SHOW

Turn off the television and have the crowd participate in a talent show. Sing "Twinkle, Twinkle Little Star," recite a poem, do a silly dance, or act out a skit with a friend. The rules of the talent show are: 1. Have fun. 2. Give everyone a chance to perform. 3. Let everyone know what a wonderful job he or she has done on the stage.

SKITTISH

Make your own skit with your child to create a comedy routine. You can base it on a favorite TV show, or be an original act.

YOU'RE ON

Pretend that you and your child are filming a scene from a movie, a talk show, or a live event. Take turns holding an imaginary video camera and a microphone. Get started with an interview about something silly, such as what's the best way to feed a monkey. Then have a demonstration of your child doing a trick. Or, capture the excitement of a cupcake-eating contest.

ACTING OUT FAIRY TALES

After reading a classic fairy tale several times, you and your child can act out some of it. Let your child be Jack in *Jack and the Beanstalk* or the Wolf in *Little Red Riding Hood*. Feel free to change the outcomes of the stories.

DANCING WITH FEELING

Share upbeat songs as well as sad music with your child. Then create a dance with your child. Do a happy jig for when you're happy. Then create a sad dance for when you're feeling sad, tired, or angry.

MUSICAL FREEZE

Dance to different types music. Make it really fun by having some one stop the music. When the music stops, freeze. When it starts back up again, dance again.

BODY MUSIC

Make different music sounds with different parts of your body. Show your child how to use your feet to stomp, your hands to clap, your mouth to sing. Try to coordinate the sounds and the body parts.

BE MY FEET

Let your child put his feet on top of yours and dance to the music.

CLAP AND STOMP

Clap your hands and stomp your feet to a popular beat, a poem, or an original song.

ANIMAL DANCE

Play dance music and ask your child to move like a monkey or a sea horse. Call out a different animal every minute or so.

FLY DANCE

How would it be if you could fly? Ask your child to spread out his wings and join you in a fly dance. Be a bird or a plane.

SNAKE MOVES

Get on the floor and move like a snake. Tuck your arms inside your shirt and slither from one side of the room to another. Challenge your child to slither about.

FACIAL EXPRESSIONS

Practice making different faces with your child in front of a mirror. Try a silly face or a scared face. Now try to copy each other's faces.

TONGUE TWISTS

Can you and your little one recite tongue twisters? Have fun with these: "Betty Bailey's batter bakes best." "Sally sells sea shells by the seashore." "Wendy wondered what the weather was." Make up your own and have a tongue-twister show.

PERFECT HARMONY

Teach your child harmony by practicing "Row, Row, Row Your Boat." Let him start the song and you chime in later.

PARADE

Line up and pretend you are part of a big parade. March around the house. Use real instruments or homemade ones.

* * * * * * * *

CONDUCTOR

Turn on classical music and have your child be the conductor of an imaginary orchestra. Explain to your child that his hands need to direct all the instruments. This will help him focus or practice self-control.

MUSIC BALL

Play your favorite music. Sit on the floor facing your child. Roll a big, soft ball back and forth to each other. Encourage her to roll the ball to the beat of the music. Pretend that the music is the ball's movement.

*   *   *   *   *   *   *   *

LIP SYNCH

Have your child pick a favorite song and pretend to be the lead singer. Give him a prop to use as a microphone.

DRESS FOR FUN

Because your love her, dress your child in her favorite getup, or as her favorite character, every third Friday of the month.

LIKE ROYALTY

Pretend you and your child are part of a royal family. You are the queen and your child is the prince or princess. Give yourselves royal names. Do a royal wave or bow.

EVENT PLANNING

Plan a wedding or other ceremony for your child's toys. Make the celebration unique by having your child plan the decorations and the refreshments.

RIDE A BROOMSTICK

Got a broom? Make a witch's broomstick or go horseback riding. Tie a cloth over a broom's bristles to make a horse's head. Take turns riding the horse and use it as a way to stir up imaginative conversation.

FAST AND SLOW

Explore the concepts of fast and slow by first clapping very slowly. Then speed up your clapping until it is very quick. Now stomp your feet very slowly. Then speed it up and stomp quickly. Now pat your tummy very slowly. Now pat it as quickly as you can. What else can you do really slowly? What can you do really fast?

HOLD THE STARE

Sit across from each other and stare silently. The first person to break the stare with a smile or laugh loses. Keep trying and whatever you do, don't laugh!

FREE WORDS

Say a word and have your child respond with the first word that comes to his mind.

PLAY OPPOSITES

Play the opposite game with your child. You begin with a word and he has to say its opposite. For example, you say, "High;" he

* * * * * * * *

says, "Low." You say, "Up;" he says, "Down." You can play this game anywhere.

OPPOSITE DAY

Once your child has mastered opposites, you can have an opposite afternoon. A "yes" really means "no," a "good" means "bad," "hello" means "good-bye," and "sad" really means "happy."

GO FOR THE BURN!

Encourage your child to share in your exercise regimen. Try doing a workout video together, walk, dance, run, or do some basic yoga. Not only will your child love the time spent with you, but he may also get the message that exercise is a key element to good health.

TIPS for BusY MomS

◎ Even if you don't have time for your daily exercise, simply romping around for about 20 minutes with your preschooler can burn about 120 calories.

CHAPTER
9
Small Gatherings

BUBBLE FUN

- $^1/_2$ cup of liquid dish soap
- 2 quarts water
- Few droplets of glycerin (available at pharmacy)

Make your own soap bubbles by mixing the liquid dish soap, water, and glycerin. Children can blow bubbles with small plastic frozen juice containers that are opened at both ends.

WATER PLAY

Fill a bucket with water and toss in some water toys.

☆　☆　☆　☆ ☆　☆　☆　☆

WATER BALLOON FUN

- An old sheet
- Water balloons

You need at least four people for this activity. Using an old sheet, bounce a few water balloons up into the air. How many balloons can you bounce into the air without breaking one?

COIN IN THE BUCKET

Fill a bucket with water. Place a quarter in it. Can your child drop a penny directly on the quarter?

SAND SCULPT

Let a group of young children play with sand in buckets. Give them muffin tins, rolling pins, and other utensils.

TELEPHONE GAME

Sit in a circle and whisper a message to the person on your left. Try something like, "Don't count your chickens before they hatch," or "If at first you don't succeed, try, try again." Have each person in the circle whisper the message. Have the last person say the message out loud. How has the original message changed? This works best with four or more people.

WE STORY

Share a story. Form a circle. Have one person can start with,

☆ ☆ ☆ ☆ ☆ ☆ ☆ ☆

"Once upon a time—." Then each person in the circle has to add a line or two to create a story with a beginning, a middle, and an end. If you've got a really dynamic group, videotape them and play the story back.

LISTEN TO ME

Polish listening skills. Sit in a circle. Pass around a large ball. Explain to the children that only one person may speak at a time. If someone wants to speak, he or she needs to hold the ball. The person with the ball has to pass it to the next person who wants to speak.

CIRCLE OF FEELINGS

Sit in a circle and make a face: happy, sad, mad, or scared. Have the others guess the mood that goes with the facial expression. Then, one by one, pass the face from person to person.

SENSES GAME

Teach the five senses to your child with this sensory game. Name something that you see, then something that you hear, then something that you taste, then something you can touch, then something you can smell. For example: a bird, a siren, an ice cream, a patch of grass, the ocean. Then have your child do the same. You're out if you can't name one of the senses.

TWINKLE, TWINKLE

Everyone loves to sing "Twinkle, Twinkle, Little Star." But add a visual element and you've really got some fun on your hands. Glue colored star shapes onto craft sticks. Give each child a star stick and then sing your hearts out.

ALPHABET FOAM LETTERS

There's so much you can do with colored foam board letters and number puzzles. Children love to put the pieces together, recite the alphabet, and, of course, jump on the spongy foam board. You can create lots of fun challenges for a small group. Put the pieces together, but out of order. Have a small group tell you which letters or numbers are out of order. Which letter is which number of the alphabet? What words can you spell in a certain amount of time? Children can work together or alone.

ALPHABET JUMP

Draw the letters of the alphabet on your driveway with colored chalk. You can draw the letters straight across or spread them out all over the place. Call out a letter and have the group run to the letter. Call out another letter. Who can find it first? If you land on the wrong letter, you're out of the game.

BODY ALPHABET

Work together to form a life-size letter. Begin with A and see if you and the group can make each letter of the alphabet with their bodies.

☆ ☆ ☆ ☆ ☆ ☆ ☆ ☆

WORDS OF THE SEASON

Does the group know the four seasons? Play this game. You say a word like, "Halloween" or "pumpkin." Someone has to call out the corresponding season (fall). Here are some season-related words to start you off:

> *Winter*—snow, ice, ski, christmas, snowman
> *Spring*—flowers, bees, egg hunt
> *Summer*—barbecue, Fourth of July, watermelon
> *Fall*—Halloween, Thanksgiving, apples

BEANBAG MITTEN

Stuff old mittens with dried beans. Sew the wrist closed with heavy yarn to make mitten beanbags.

BEANBAG TARGET

Make a beanbag target out of a large cardboard box. Have the children decorate it with a silly picture on one side. Cut out several holes. Try to throw the beanbag through the holes.

FOUR IDEAS FOR BEANBAG FUN

1 Toss a two-color beanbag up in the air and guess with the children which color will land faceup.
2 Have everyone balance a beanbag on their head as they walk around. See who can keep it there the longest. If this

is too easy, you can make it more challenging by placing a
book on their head and then put the beanbag on top of it.

3 Get on all fours and race with a few beanbags on your
back. If a beanbag falls, you're out.

4 Draw x's and o's on beanbags with colored chalk and play
tic-tac-toe.

HULA HOOP THROW

Hold a plastic hula hoop upright and let the group toss soft
small balls through it. Keep score.

BALLS IN BINS

> • An empty plastic laundry basket
> • A small wicker basket
> • Coffee cans

In the backyard, set up an empty plastic laundry basket, a small
wicker basket, and coffee cans. Gather a bunch of balls in different sizes. Set up a point system for each of the bins and have
everyone try to toss the balls into the bins.

FACE PAINTING FUN

Go ahead and paint your face and while you're at it, paint the
faces of everyone in the neighborhood. Invest in a child's face
painting kit and spend some time practicing. Make simple hearts,
butterflies, and flowers on small cheeks. Or, be bold and make

lion, puppy, and clown faces. If you become good at face painting, you'll be very useful at birthday parties and town fairs, and you'll be a hot commodity when you have school-age children.

WORKING TOGETHER

Demonstrate cooperation by making a well-oiled machine with a few children. Be a popcorn popper or a traffic light. Have one child begin with a sound and a movement. Then have another child add another sound and movement to the machine. Keep going until you have everyone working together. Videotape your well-oiled machine.

LINKED AT THE ELBOW

Have two children stand back to back with their elbows linked. Tell the children to sit down without letting go of each other. Then stand up without letting go of each other. See which two-some can do it the fastest.

GROUP PICTURE

Lay down a drop cloth and have the children create a mural together based on a theme. Some favorite themes include: rainbows, sea life, monsters, trees, and flowers.

FRIENDSHIP BRACELETS

- Yarn
- Beads

Make bracelets using colored yarn and beads. Friends can present them to each other and make up their own friendship handshakes.

OBSTACLES

Create in the backyard a course of tables to crawl under, hula hoops to crawl through, and piles of pillows to climb over. Keep it fun and safe. If you've got a small group of children, you can put them in teams and then time them. Who has the best score?

BIG BOX

Next time you have a large delivery, save the box. It will provide hours of free play for a group of children. Set the box on the floor and let them creep, crawl, and hide inside it.

RACE CAR

> • Large cardboard box
> • Tape
> • Markers
> • Streamers and ribbons

Make your very own race car that you can step into and pretend to ride. Just open a large cardboard box, bend it in half and tuck one side under the rest to form a triangle shape. Now decorate the box with markers. Tape four colorful paper plates to look like wheels. Attach colored streamers to the back of the race car. Attach two ribbons from the front of the car to the back of the car to act as shoulder straps. Number each car and race away.

LIMBO

Tape two empty wrapping-paper tubes together. Decorate it with colored paper, rubber stamps, stickers, or markers. Use it as a limbo stick and see how low everyone can go.

SCAVENGER HUNT

Give each child a list of items to find in the backyard or playroom. Your list can be made up of a combination of pictures and words. Have them search for objects such as a red ball, a book, a sock, a spoon, a square shape, and maybe a toy surprise. Give each child a small basket to carry his or her items in. See who can gather the most items.

• Playing games with other children is a great opportunity for your child to learn good sportsmanship. Let him experience what it's like to win and lose. Always stress to him the old adage, "It's not whether you win or lose, but how you play the game."

ROW IT

Have everyone climb aboard the S.S. _____ (fill in the name of your child). Give each child a wooden spoon to act as an oars while everyone sings, "Row, Row, Row Your Boat."

DREAM TOWN

Draw a town with colored chalk. The town could be real or pretend. Make a candy land, an amusement park, or a shopping center. When it's done, have everyone walk through the town.

SIMPLE SIMON SAYS

Encourage the grown-ups to play along with the children. When you're Simon, you face the crowd and instruct players on what to do: flap your elbows, pat your tummy, hop on one foot. The only rule is, players should only do it if Simon actually says, "Simon Says—." If Simon tells you to do something without the Simon Says, you're out. The winner gets a turn at being Simon.

PLAY KIDS' MUSIC

There's a ton of fun songs and games out there that encourage dance, movement, and creative thinking. Buy a few CDs and swap them with your friends.

CHAPTER 10

Rainy Day Fun

* * * * * * * *

RAINY DAY PICTURES

Using paint and markers, draw shapes and lines on a piece of paper. Place your picture out in the rain for a few minutes. Dry it out and then examine your art.

LAUNDRY SHUTTLE

Give your child a ride in a plastic laundry basket. Tie a rope through the side handle and take her around the play area.

SUGAR PLAY

Instead of sandbox play, fill a large bowl with sugar or rice. Let your child pour, sift, and play with it.

STEPPING STONES

Scatter colored paper plates across a room. Now pretend that the carpet is a brook. You can only get from one end of the brook to the other by stepping on the plates.

COTTON BALL RACES

- Cotton balls
- Plastic straws
- A table and two chairs

Sit next to your child at one end of the table. Each of you has a cotton ball and a straw. When you say go, each player has to get the cotton ball pass the opposite side of the table by blowing it through the straw. The player who blows the cotton ball off the table first wins the round. Play ten rounds.

RAINY DAY BOX

Keep a rainy day box in your closet. Fill it with scarves, hats, gloves, shawls, costumes, rubber noses, wigs, and other fun stuff.

TWO FINGERS

Do a two-fingers-in-the-air dance as you sing a rhyme. Sing it slow, then fast; sing it softly, then loudly. When your child least expects it, let your fingers land for a quick belly tickle. Then repeat as many times as you want.

UPSIDE DOWN

Hang upside down from your bed or living room couch with your child to gain a new perspective. Ask, "What would things be like if upside down was right-side up? and "How do things look when you're upside down?" For fun, pretend that you're bats by making bat sounds.

RUBBER BAND BALLS

- All the rubber bands you can get your hands on

Make a real ball from wrapping rubber bands around each other. Twist a rubber band around several others and keep going until you've got a ball. Use colored rubber bands to make the ball colorful. When your ball is done, think about how many rubber bands it took to make.

TOY HOSPITAL

Play doctor and nurse to your child's dolls. Use shoe boxes for the beds and washcloths for the blankets. Wrap bandages around the dolls' wounds. Use a medical kit, if you have one. Or, use a straw for a thermometer.

SKATE!

- Carpeted area
- Sheets of wax paper
- Rubber bands
- Masking tape

Anyone for ice skating? Outline a large area of carpet with masking tape to be the designated skating rink. Give each skater two large pieces of wax paper. Gather the waxed paper around each ankle amd fasten with colorful rubber bands. Play music and let the skaters skate.

*   *   *   *   *   *   *   *

BOWLING INSIDE

> • Six empty plastic soft drink bottles
> • A soft squishy ball

Line up the six bottles at one of end of the hallways for a indoor
bowling game. For added fun, tape a word, number, or letter to
each plastic bottle. When each bottle falls, have your child identify the word, number, or letter on it.

TIME IT

Teach your child about the concept of time. Using a stopwatch,
or a watch with a second hand, find out how long it takes for
your child to get dressed, take a bath, brush her teeth, eat an
apple, or draw a picture.

RAINMAKER

Show your child how you can make it rain inside the house. Boil
a pot of water. Fill a pie plate with ice cubes and hold it above
the pot. When the steam comes in contact with the cool pie
plate, water droplets will form and sprinkle back into the pot
like rain.

MIRROR IMAGE

Face your child. Tell him that he is supposed to imagine that he
is looking in the mirror. As you move, he has to copy your

movements and expressions. After a while, switch so that you be your child's mirror.

PEEP AND CHIRP

Pretend that you are birds on a spring morning. Speak in bird language by chirping, squawking, or peeping your way through lunch.

LEFT, RIGHT

Teach your child left and right by playing a game of accessorize. You will need a lot of bangles, bracelets, and some shoes. Ask your child to put this shoe on your right foot, or put this red bracelet on your left hand.

ANOTHER LEFT, RIGHT

You can also teach your child left and right by looking for a beauty mark or freckle on her face. If she has none, you can put a little lipstick mark one of her cheeks.

COUNT IT

Count the number of doorknobs, television sets, telephones, windows, beds, and lamps in your house.

PENNY ROLLS

Count pennies and make penny rolls. Then bring it to the bank with your child.

OUTLINES

Make outlines of shapes. Then ask your child to color the circles yellow, the squares green, and the triangles pink.

ART SPACE

Create an art studio for your child. Make sure it is in a place that she can make messy. Have smocks, paints, brushes, crayons, markers, and paper on hand. Let your child decorate the space with her artwork.

HOUSE BOX

Use a large cardboard box to play house. Cut out the doors and windows for your child. Help him design and decorate the house with paper curtains, a welcome mat, and pictures on the wall.

* * * * * * * *

WATER MUSIC

> Four tall drinking glasses
> Metal spoon

Pour 1 inch (2 ¹/₂ cm) of water in the first glass, 2 inches (5 cm) in the second glass, 3 inches (7 ¹/₂ cm) in the third glass, and 4 inches (10 cm) in the fourth glass. Line up the glasses and tap gently on each glass with the spoon. Notice how the amount of water in the glass changes the sound in your water xylophone.

DRAW TO MUSIC

Play any kind of music and let your child draw to the rhythm, the tempo, and the mood. Try Vivaldi's "The Four Seasons" or Tchaikovsky's "The Nutcracker Suite" for amazing results.

SHARE A HOBBY

Share your hobby with your child. He can sit beside you as the two of you read or he can help you decorate flowers.

CARD STORE

Using a variety of paper, pens, stickers, rubber stamps, stencils, or even the computer, create different cards with your child. Thank-you notes, greeting cards, holiday cards, and birthday cards will always come in handy.

SECRET MESSAGES

- Two paper cups
- String
- Pencil

Punch a small hole in the center of each paper cup bottom using a pencil point. Thread a string through each from the bottom. Knot the ends so the string won't slip out. You and your child can send and receive secret messages.

✳   ✳   ✳   ✳   ✳   ✳   ✳   ✳

MAPMAKER

Make a map using paper and colored markers. Have your child draw a special place like her bedroom, daycare center, or a friend's toy room. Help her identify the doorways and furniture. She can also color in the different objects on the map or write in key words.

MAPMAKER TWO

Take your child's mapmaking skills to the next level. Have him create a map from your home to the local park or super market. Don't forget streets. Once he's done, wait until the rain stops and then take a walk with him using the map . Check if anything's missing. Applaud him on his memory.

TIPS for BusY MomS

- ◎ If you're taking your child to the movies on a rainy Saturday, resist the urge to stuff him with candy just keep him happy. Let him watch the movie without popcorn every once in a while or he may associate movies with filling up on popcorn and candy.

- ◎ Let your child bring out your silly, gamey self. Embrace those moments when you can actually feel like a child again!

- ◎ Your child never gets tired of asking why. Learn from her. Ask why, why, and why—and don't forget why not.

✳ *Rainy Day Fun* ✳

CHAPTER 11
Mini-Holiday Guide

✻   ✻   ✻   ✻   ✻   ✻   ✻   ✻

TIPS for BusY MomS

- During holidays, busy moms go into overdrive. They are often stuck in the kitchen perfecting traditional dishes, shopping for gifts, cleaning in preparation for company, or making crafts with their kids in an effort to make each holiday memorable and festive. Slow down! Take a moment to recall your favorite holiday moments when you were a child. What made these times so special? Go back in time and try to remember the smells, the sounds, the colors, and the holiday table. Share some of these memories with your child.

- When you celebrate your holidays with your family, try to include your child in the planning and in the preparation. Make up your own traditions as you go along and relish the memories.

READ ALL ABOUT IT

There are children's books about every holiday. Read them (even the books about the holidays that your family doesn't celebrate) to your child. Talk with her about how the holiday evolved and what it means to different families. Consider making a holiday bookshelf in your house for these books.

REACH INTO THE COMMUNITY

Volunteer to read holiday stories at your child's library. This will give you and your child an opportunity to create a special event that can be enjoyed by the entire community. Afterwards, you can have the children draw their own pictures for the holiday.

YOUR OWN HOLIDAY BOOK

You and your child can write poems and stories about the holidays you celebrate.

CELEBRATE THE WHOLE SEASON

Focus not only on the occasion, but the season it falls under. For example, for Halloween, teach your child about the harvest. Buy pumpkins, gourds, apples, and other traditional fruits of the season.

MAKE INVITATIONS

If you will be entertaining at your house, let your child help you make and send out invitations. You can write the message and he can add the finishing touches, such as a border of fingerprints.

FROM THE HEART

Make your own holiday cards from heart-shaped paper. Write sweet messages and let your child illustrate them with x's (kisses) and o's (hugs).

* * * * * * * *

SEND OUT CARDS

If you're sending out holiday greeting cards, encourage your little one to help. She can help you put the card in the envelope, seal the envelope, and decorate it with stickers. As you complete each card, your child can check it off your list.

GOING SHOPPING

Try to do the bulk of your shopping while your little one is having some Daddy or Grandparent Time. But, by all means, bring your child with you for a small dose of holiday shopping. Point out all the holiday trimmings and keep your child actively involved in the shopping. Let him choose between the furry slippers and the polka-dot gloves for Aunt Gussie.

MARBLEIZED GIFT

- A box
- Construction paper
- Tempera paint in at least two colors
- Three or four marbles

Make marbleized paintings with your child. They make beautiful pictures or fun wrapping paper. Place a piece of construction paper in the box. Pour in a tablespoon of two different-colored paints. (Green and red are excellent choices for Christmas. Pink and red are great for Valentine's Day.) Place the marbles into the box and let your child gently rock the box so that the marbles go up, down, and all around the paper. When your child decides that the work is done, hang it to dry.

For a special grandparent's gift, have your child do three of these paintings in the same color scheme. Then frame each one for a fabulous wall display.

HOLIDAY ORNAMENTS

Let your child make simple ornaments for the holidays. Teach her about the colors that are associated with each holiday.

PHOTO ORNAMENTS

- Several photos of your child
- Coffee mug
- Pencil
- Scissors
- Cardstock
- Glue
- Hole punch
- Ribbon
- Magnet

Your child can make either photo ornaments for a Christmas tree and/or photo magnets for any other holiday. Let her choose several photos from the year, or you can take new photos of her dressed for the occasion. Use a coffee mug to trace a circle onto each photo. Cut the photo out and glue it onto a slightly larger circle of cardstock. Make a hole at the top and thread a ribbon through it. Tie it to your tree. To make a photo magnet, glue the magnet to the back of the photo. Wrap it up in colored tissue paper and let your child give her gift.

SOAP SHAPES

- Bar of soap
- Large bowl
- $1/4$ cup water
- 2 drops of food coloring
- Cookie cutters
- Kitchen grater

Finely grate the bar of soap in a big bowl. Add water and coloring. Mix well and spoon into cookie cutters. Pack the mixture firmly and let it dry overnight. Wrap the soaps in netting, or tissue paper, and tie it with a colorful ribbon.

You can make scented soap by adding a few drops of essential oil available from craft or health food stores.

SING IT

Let your child perform singing telegrams (live or through the telephone) to his loved ones for birthdays, Valentine's Day, or any day.

CHOCOLATE SPOONS

- Chocolate
- Colored plastic spoons
- Colored sprinkles
- Wrapping materials

Dip colored plastic spoons in melted chocolate and top with colored sprinkles. Wrap each in colored cellophane and tie it with a ribbon.

❆　　❆　　❆　　❆　　　　❆　　❆　　❆　　❆

BAKE IT

Bake cookies in heart shapes and let your child decorate them with colored sugar. Wrap the cookies in clear bags lined with pink and red tissue paper. Let your child give the cookies to friends and relatives.

MAKING PLATTERS

When it comes to the food, there's a lot that a young child can do. She can help you make a vegetable platter, put chips into a bowl, and place it on a table. She can arrange a platter of cheese and crackers. She can sprinkle toppings, like grated cheese, onto a dish.

FOOD PATTERN

When your child is helping you put food onto a tray, encourage him to make a pattern: green pepper, red pepper, cherry tomato, carrot, and celery. See if he can continue the pattern.

ART TABLE

If you have lots of young children coming, set up the kids' table with a large piece of butcher paper over it. Hand out crayons and let the children decorate the table with pictures reprsenting the occasion.

LEAVE IT

Let your child collect beautifully-colored leaves and laminate them. Dress up a holiday table with the leaves.

TURKEY RACES

- White paper plates
- Scissors
- Colored feathers
- Brightly-colored construction paper
- Glue
- Staples
- Shoelaces

This Thanksgiving activity is ideal for a young group of children. First, make the turkeys out of simple white paper plates. Decorate each with colored feathers or pieces of brightly-colored construction paper to make instant turkeys. Staple a pair of shoelaces to the edges of the plate. Have each player "tie on a turkey." Set up a starting point and a finishing point. Have two players race at a time like turkeys: their hands folded under their arms while making, "Gobble, Gobble," sounds.

TURKEY SONG

Make colored turkeys with paper plates and colored feathers. Attach them to craft sticks. Give each child a different-colored turkey, then sing, "Where is red turkey. Where is red turkey?" The child holding the red turkey stands up and says, "Here I am, gobble, gobble." Sing until all the different-colored turkeys get a chance to stand. For Easter, you can make paper rabbits.

PIN THE WATTLE

What's that red, fleshy flap that hangs under the turkey beak? A wattle. Draw a large turkey on a poster board. Have your child color it in and glue feathers on it. Then make a wattle out of red paper. Attach a piece of two-sided tape to the wattle and play "Pin the Wattle on the Turkey" with your guests. For Christmas, you can change the game to "Pin the Red Nose on Rudolph."

HALLOWEEN CANDY EXCHANGE

So that your child doesn't get sick from eating all the candy (or if she has a food allergy, say, to peanuts), take all the wrapped candy she collects from trick-or-treating, and let her trade it in for a bag of goodies: small toys, stickers, pens, erasers, books, and other trinkets.

TIPS for Busy Moms

◎ For gatherings, make sure you have enough healthy and acceptable snacks on hand. A ready supply of fruits, vegetables, and other snacks will decrease the likelihood of a food-related problem.

HALLOWEEN HOST

Consider letting your child help you open the door to trick-or-treaters. Have him appear in a costume and let him give out the treats. Or, you can host your own neighborhood parade and costume contest.

HAUNTED SOUNDS

Create an assortment of spooky sounds. All you need is a box of instruments: bells, triangles, rhythm sticks, rattles—even cans filled with dried beans. Work together to imagine Halloween creatures and the haunted sounds that go with each creature.

PUMPKIN POWER

Have a pumpkin-decorating party. Carve or paint the pumpkins and let the children on your block vote on the most creative pumpkins.

TALK ABOUT IT

When it's all over, spend some time talking about the holiday with your child. Ask her what foods she liked and didn't like.

Have talk about some of the activities she did for the occasion. Also, remind her of the guests that came and try to get her to describe each person.

MAKE THANK-YOU CARDS

Let your child help design and decorate thank-you cards by using rubber stamps, stickers, glue, and glitter. Read aloud each message that you write to each person. Let your little helper seal each card.

MAKE A SCRAPBOOK

You and your child can create a unique scrapbook of holiday moments. Let your child fill the book with photos and captions. He can draw pictures and create stories about the highlights of the day. Write the holiday menu. Include crafts, stories, and songs that made the holiday so wonderful. Share the scrapbook with him next year as the holiday approaches again. This will give him a refresher course on what to expect.

Acknowledgments

A special thanks to two creative and spirited teachers, Jackie Ritch and Helen Calamari. Much appreciation to my old friend Staci Lambert and my new friend Lisa Irving Trader. And a hearty thanks to the joyful mamas of PACT (Parent and Child Together). With bits of humor and grace, you all make mommyhood look like a piece of cake.

About the Author

Jamie Kyle McGillian is the author of *The Kids' Money Book* (Sterling), *Sidewalk Chalk: Outdoor Fun and Games* (Sterling), *Tugs & Hugs: A Recipe for Social and Emotional Growth* (Rigby), and On The *Job with a Firefighter: Neighborhood Guardian* (Barrons Juveniles). Before becoming a busy mom, she was an editor at Sesame Workshop for seven years. A former founding editor of Creative Classroom magazine, Jamie is the recipient of an EdPress Award. She teaches writing to third, fourth, and fifth graders. She lives with her husband and two little girls in Westchester County, New York.

Index